T0417582

ASK THE WITCH

Edited by
FRANCESCA MATTEONI

Illustrations by
SIMONE PACE

ROCKPOOL

CONTENTS

THE RIDER WAITE SMITH TAROT DECK — 4

THE HISTORY AND THE STORIES OF TAROT CARDS — 4

WITCHES IN THE TAROT CARDS: HOW TO USE THIS DECK — 8

SYMBOLS OF THE MAJOR ARCANA — 11

SYMBOLS OF THE MINOR ARCANA — 57

READING AND INTERPRETING THE TAROT CARDS — 114

THE WITCHES' MESSAGES — 119

THE RIDER WAITE SMITH TAROT DECK

What you are holding in your hand is a magical object, a deck of Tarot cards that contains the stories and symbols of the Rider Waite Smith (RWS) system. The first RWS deck was published in England in 1910 by the editor, Rider, based on indications from Arthur E. Waite and illustrated by Pamela Colman Smith. Both Waite and Smith belonged to the Golden Dawn, a secret, initiatory society whose members strove to achieve a more authentic awareness of reality through the study of ancient, esoteric writings and through individually experimenting with new avenues of knowledge.

The Tarot deck is, then, a compendium of knowledge and intuitions in 78 images. It can be read as a book whose plot is ever changing, depending on the arrangement of its elements.

THE HISTORY AND THE STORIES OF TAROT CARDS

The Tarot cards are a game, so let's begin by shuffling the cards to our liking and journeying back in time toward their origins. Our first shuffle takes us back to the Renaissance courts of Italy, when the Tarot cards appeared as the four classic suits combined with important figures of the era that represented the empire, religion, and natural events such as death, as well as heavenly bodies. Then, Tarot cards reflected an era in which the spiritual realm and the realm of physical existence were closely interconnected. Individual characteristics were subject to the influence of heavenly bodies, royal power descended from the divine, sin was the leading cause of every disease, and love transformed loved ones into angels while demons were always ready to interfere in relational balances. A second shuffle takes us back to the turn of the nineteenth century when the game started being used for divination purposes—a way to contact the divine in order to predict the future. When we shuffle the cards a third time, we find ourselves in London, at a meeting of the Golden Dawn, where divination becomes a magical experience used to interpret ourselves and the world around us. Today, the RWS deck, as well as a variety of other illustrated decks, is readily available on bookstore shelves. For some it is an object of beauty and art, while for others it is a tool to be used to read the future, to invent a story, to stimulate our imagination, or to find comfort and company in its images. What does the deck consist of?

The 78 cards are divided into two main groups. The first group, the most prominent and eye-catching, is made of the 22 cards of the Major Arcana. The numbered cards begin with 0, The Fool (which in antiquity had no number, just as number XIII, Death, had no name), and end with The World, number XXI. Before us, we have great forces that regulate and sway life on both a cosmic and personal level. If we arrange them in numeric order, they trace the course of a lifetime. In the Fool, we have potential, and in the Magician, the ability to activate it. In the High Priestess, there is the receptiveness to the world; in the Empress, creation. In the Emperor, we have authority and will. The Hierophant holds traditional education, while in the Lovers we find love and its choices. In the Chariot, there is ambition, and in Strength, courage. There is solitary faith in one's own ideas in the Hermit. The Wheel of Fortune has alternating strokes of fate. Justice holds the moral order ascribed to things. In the Hanged Man, we have sacrifice and obstacles, and in Death, the constant transformation of everything. Temperance holds the compassion we need, for ourselves and for others. In the Devil, there are passion, temptation, and the road to perdition. The Tower is the sudden collapse and the brutal, liberating truth. The Star is hope, and in the Moon are night dreams, wildness, deceit, and the unpredictable. The Sun holds success and joy, and in Justice we have vocation, reawakening, and acknowledged worth. In the World, there is that vast, terrible, joyous place where everything begins, is completed, and then begins anew.

To be clear, the numbers are simply a helpful formality. The order can vary and we may find a case, for example, that begins with Justice and ends with the Hermit; it is up to us to tie the threads of sense between one card and another.

The remaining cards make up the Minor Arcana. They reflect challenges, meetings, and daily changes. They are divided into four suits, Wands, Cups, Swords, and Pentacles, that represent the four universal elements of Fire, Water, Air, and Earth and their spiritual connections.

Wands are connected to creativity, new projects and personal desires, inspiration and passion in following one's purposes, impulse, vision and progress, the defense of personal values, and action. They suggest resources that seem infinite: dynamism, exuberance, and enthusiasm.

Cups delve into our souls with sensitivity, examining our relationships and demonstrating our pure fragility where the world leaves its mark. Here, where we find our loves and friendships, creativity blends with empathy and the deep desire to touch the heart of others and to understand and welcome them.

Swords are connected to the mind. They evoke truth and revelation, opening the way for communications, thought, reason, and the direct solution to problems. They indicate the ability for analysis and long-term planning, trust in one's own actions, intelligence and language, cunning and survival.

Pentacles symbolize wealth and the manifestation of material things, from the body to the world. They speak to us of health and prosperity, work, dedication to endeavors and loved ones, family, reciprocity and generosity, economic issues, a sense of responsibility and care, and determination in carrying out our dreams.

Each of the four suits has cards numbered from ace to ten, from the original power to the depletion (or completion) of the suit. Each also has 4 cards representing figures of the court: the Page, the Knight, the Queen, and the King. These are the most difficult to decipher and may indicate temperaments and characters just like those of real people we meet. It is true that the cards of the Major Arcana indicate points of crucial change or issues regarding our soul, but those of the Minor Arcana also have a great importance since it is the daily occurrences that can change the flow of our days with meetings and adventures that feed our memory.

WITCHES IN THE TAROT CARDS: HOW TO USE THIS DECK

This deck is based on the RWS system but with a unique trait: it is full of witches from all over the globe, traveling on brooms, in their cauldrons, coming out of the trees and dark waters, brandishing blades, and hiding bags of magic herbs, all the time enhancing the symbolism of the Arcana with their spells.

In the 22 cards of the Major Arcana are witches that may be famous or that we may be meeting for the first time. They are goddesses, spirits, great enchantresses, woodland creatures, creatures of the oceans and of other worlds that can be perceived on the edge of our own. But they are also mortals, considered witches because of traditions and the time they lived in. They have advice for us that they are willing to reveal if we will heed them; and although the witches represented here are all female, we wanted to leave a certain amount of ambiguity in the Minor Arcana so that everyone can identify with them.

After all, women are not the sole proprietors of female power. We can speak of female power each time we attempt to be equal to others rather than to excel, but the witches are contradictory and some of them will surprise you with a decisive attitude that many would describe as masculine. Only one thing is certain: when we talk about magic, we have to get used to standing at the threshold, waiting to see who will come, knowing that wisdom and surprise give life to the most varied of beings. A primrose sprouting from a devastated field is no less important a messenger than an ancient queen returning home.

All the witches in the deck encourage you to look beyond their image and scrutinize the details. They invite you to experience the nearness of life in all its shapes, with a curious inclination for listening, beginning with those closest to us, namely, other animals. In fact, it is well known that witches have familiars, or animal companions, who share their arts. Sometimes they themselves turn into animals or strange creatures as you can see, especially in the cards of the Court, where each witch is represented with her familiar. For example, Knights are depicted as witches traveling in the sky, riding winged animals that are related to the suit's element. Kings, on the other hand, appear as incarnations of the Ancestors, those from whom we came and to whom we will return, and manifest their element in all its power. The animal is never less important than the witch is, so we must be ready to follow it and understand its worth.

Witches love to weave secret plots almost as much as they love to braid the manes of horses and run wildly with hares at night. That is why there are four hidden stories in the deck, one for each suit, that progress from the Minor Arcana through the Court to the Major Arcana, or vice versa. How will you know them? Follow the familiars, particularly the cat, the heron, the wren, and the deer. Try to identify them, consider the events and how they are linked, and imagine the cards in the order of past, present, and future. The stories are open and the last word is yours. Then create your own magical story. Shuffle the deck, pick a card, dream, and remember the 79th card, the one that is not there. When you are able to turn that card over, it will welcome you with a familiar friendly air, winking at you as though from the other side of the mirror.

SYMBOLS OF THE MAJOR ARCANA

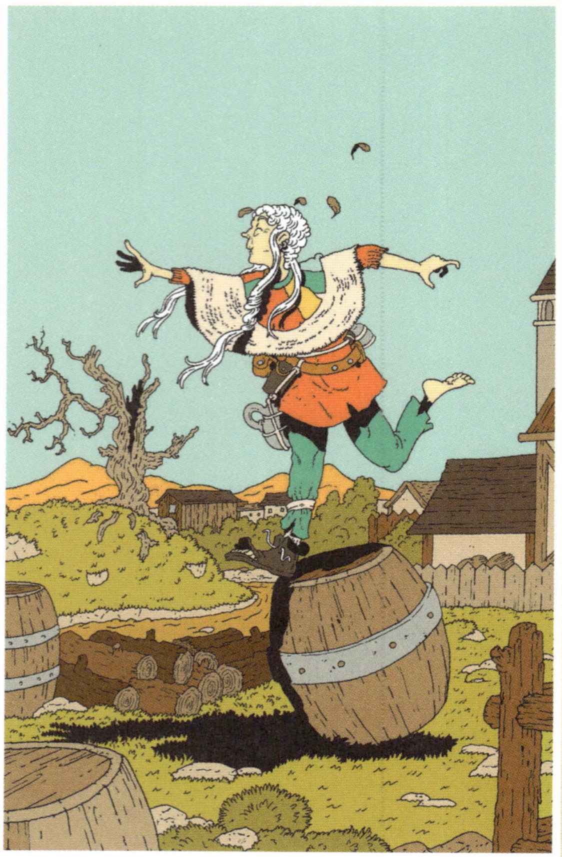

0 - THE FOOL

CRAZY JANE

Next door to the home of the Irish poet and magician, William Butler Yeats, lived an elderly woman who was a bit mad. Because of her age and her mental state, she was very straightforward in expressing her thoughts. She was the poet's inspiration when he created the figure of Crazy Jane, the central character in a series of poems; she was old, promiscuous, witchlike, infantile, and daring. She spoke to God about her love and fearlessly addressed the bishop, the symbol of conformity and morality. "Fair and foul are near of kin / And fair needs foul," she told him in one poem. "For nothing can be sole or whole / That has not been rent." In other words, to exist means being willing to become unexpected things as well as their opposites and to discover beauty where most see uselessness, knowing that rips and wounds let the light come in. This extraordinary lady of the vagabonds is our introduction to the card of the Fool, the free and infinite potential in each of us. She is the forerunner of the witches, goddesses, and women we will meet, and she holds them all in her rags, just as the number zero holds all the other numbers in its cosmic circle. Jane seems to sing out: "Recognize the magic in rivulets, in the patterns in the dust and in the stubborn trust that the heart has in life." There is a fragile balance between the sky and the earth, a game of leaves in the wind. It takes only an instant to fall, the same as it does to fly.

THE WITCH'S SPELLS

<u>POSITIVE</u>: potential, innocence, imagination, freedom

<u>NEGATIVE</u>: aimlessness, superficiality, thoughtlessness

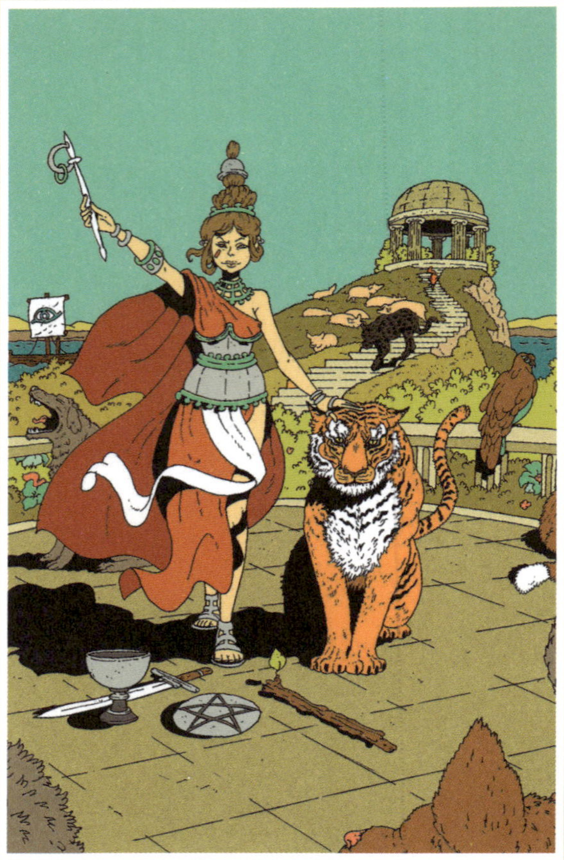

I - THE MAGICIAN

CIRCE

Circe, the daughter of the Sun, lives on an island with wolves, lions, and other wild beasts that obey her. When Ulysses landed on the island with his men, she invited them to feast with her and turned them into pigs. When the only man to escape warned Ulysses, he confronted Circe with the help of the god Hermes, who gave him the gift of immunity to the spell with a protective herb. Ulysses triumphed over Circe and became her lover. The story is one of a confrontation between equals with clever and opposing minds that come together in the end, under Hermes, the patron of thieves, magicians, and travelers. Circe is able to transform the men into beasts because she knows their vices; she seduces them, playing on their weaknesses. Living on her own has taught her to defend herself, not by using brute force but by studying and anticipating her enemy. She is able to speak the language of the animals. The attention of the Magician is directed to the origin and the consequences of desire, creating unity among various energies. Seated next to Circe is an Asian tiger, an animal absent from the epic tale but perfect for the card, with its ability to move both on land, as it hunts, and in the water, as an able swimmer. With one hand Circe points to the sky with her scepter, and with the other she pets the tiger. Above as below, in the mind as in the body, magic aims at the center, at the genuine ... deception after deception.

THE WITCH'S SPELLS

POSITIVE: concentration, resources, ingeniousness, direction of intent

NEGATIVE: wasted talent, manipulation, lack of scruples

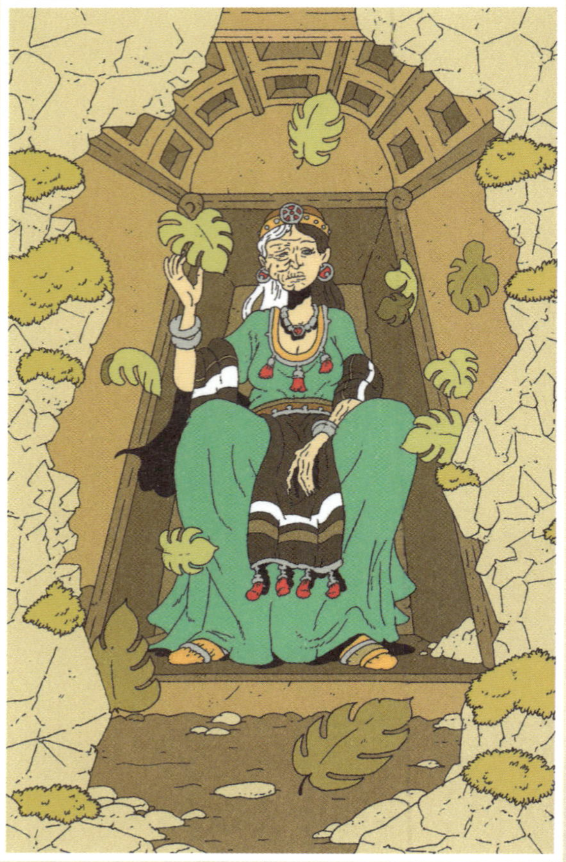

II - THE HIGH PRIESTESS

CUMAEAN SIBYL

Ancient stories say that Lake Avernus, near Naples, was the door to the world beyond the grave. Near the lake is the cave of the Sibyl, who lives on the threshold between the world of the living and that of the dead, transcending the dualism between the two. She is granted immortality by the god Apollo, who fell in love with her, but she does not retain her youth. Though her knowledge of the outside world stays that of the young girl dedicated to the god, her inner wisdom grows as she assimilates the stories of the past and the intuitions of future destinies. She writes her prophecies on leaves because while knowledge is fragile in the common language, it is strong in the inner space of premonitions, of contact with the forces of nature, and of listening to time and to its silence. Her body becomes a hindrance and shrinks like a leaf to the point of completely disappearing into her voice, an ancestral echo among the rocks. The Sybil introduces the card's mysteries of the High Priestess, who shows us the line between the visible and the invisible, between thought and subconscious. The High Priestess talks to shadows, draws her answers from the deep. She is obscure and mysterious like something important we have lost in a dream and breathlessly chase after. At times, meeting her may signal difficulty in daily social communications, but often it is an invitation to introspection, a journey into our spirit, in the company of ancestors.

THE WITCH'S SPELLS

POSITIVE: intuitive truth, inner voice, mediation, foresight

NEGATIVE: repression of feelings, difficulty in communication

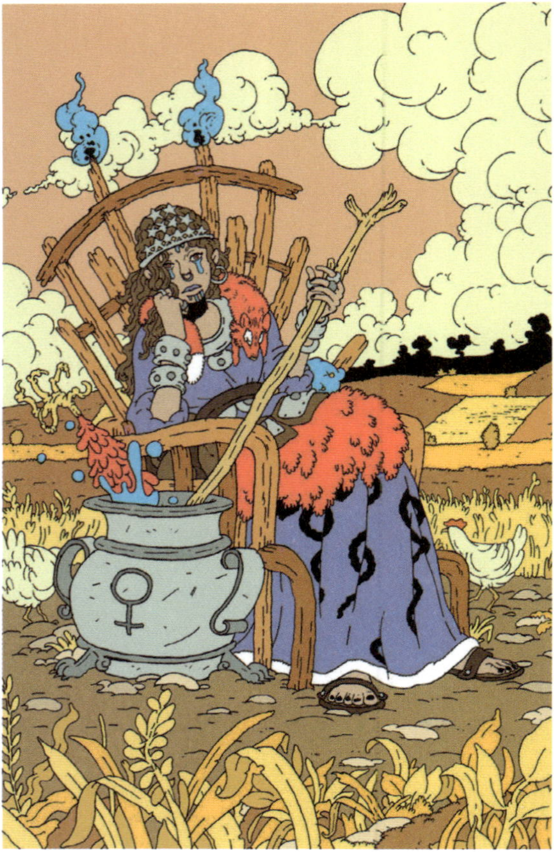

III - THE EMPRESS

CERIDWEN

In Welsh legends, Ceridwen is remembered at times as a powerful sorceress, and at others as a goddess. She was able to unleash extraordinary powers as she walked among mortals, sharing their passions and desires. Her son, Morfran, was the ugliest child ever born, so Ceridwen decided to compensate for his horrible aspect by granting him a special gift. She prepared a magic potion in her cauldron that cooked for a year and a day, the first three drops of which would bestow wisdom and the rest of which would be a lethal poison. As the blind old man Morda and the young Gwion watched over the cauldron, three drops of the potion splashed onto Gwion's thumb. He licked them off, inciting the terrible wrath of the sorceress. He tried to escape by transforming himself into different things; and when, at last, he turned himself into a grain of wheat, Ceridwen turned herself into a chicken and ate him. He began to grow in her womb and after he was born, he grew to be the famous bard, Taliesin, the personification of poetry and prophecy. In her cauldron, the Empress Ceridwen had cooked the terrestrial asset of knowledge, which, through poetry, became the art of seeing the secret nature of things. She is the protector of affection, a dispenser of a magic that transforms all of those who receive it. The Empress's greatest teaching is not one of personal power but one of completing one's mission, just as a son is to his mother.

THE WITCH'S SPELLS

<u>POSITIVE:</u> creativity, motherhood, healing, beauty, dedication

<u>NEGATIVE:</u> laziness, excess, envy, sterility, chaos

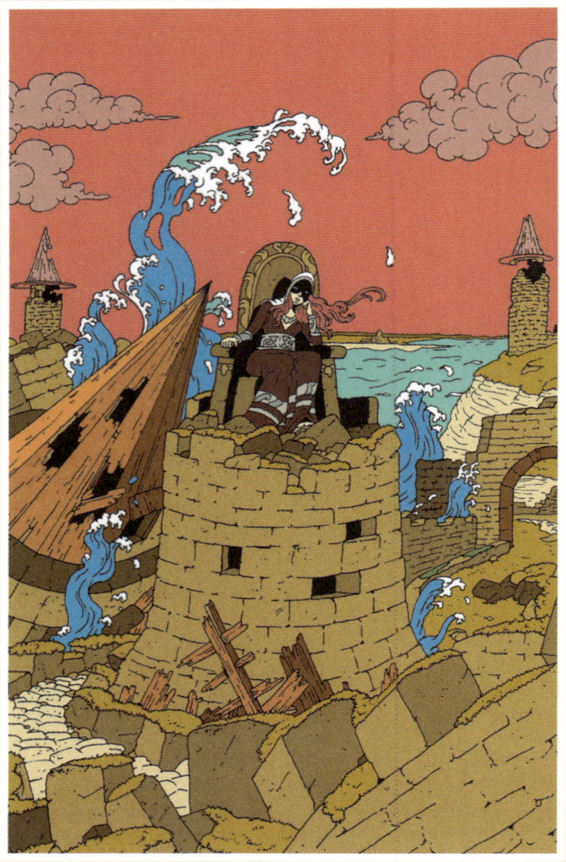

IV - THE EMPEROR

MORGAN LE FAY

According to Celtic tradition, sovereignty is bestowed through matrimony or a sexual relationship with the goddess who protects and embodies the territory that the future king will govern. As such, sovereignty is a pact that will always remind the king that the land is vast and alive and destined to last longer than any success he may accomplish. If his reign is just and compassionate, it is not an achievement, but rather a concession. Many of Morgan's transformations can be summed up in this myth: the fairy, the goddess, and the woman who observes from afar, who accompanies King Arthur in his rise to power, who opposes him until his fall, and who ultimately comes to his aid, transporting him to the island of Avalon, where he sleeps the sleep of a hero. In the most famous tales of King Arthur, Morgan is his older half sister, the daughter born of Igraine and the Duke of Cornwall. She is human, but she wants to learn magic; or perhaps her origins are those of a fairy that bind her to the land. She becomes a mother figure for Arthur, but she is also a lover, an enemy, and a healer, with no contradiction since the gift of power calls for a great sense of responsibility and is harsh and generous at the same time. The card of the Emperor represents the basis of power, primitive and rebellious like the ocean; solid like the will of those who have no fear of defeat, who cultivate it and prepare to accept it, knowing that everything is temporary.

THE WITCH'S SPELLS

POSITIVE: willpower, authority, decisiveness, a guiding figure

NEGATIVE: oppression, authoritarianism, lack of control

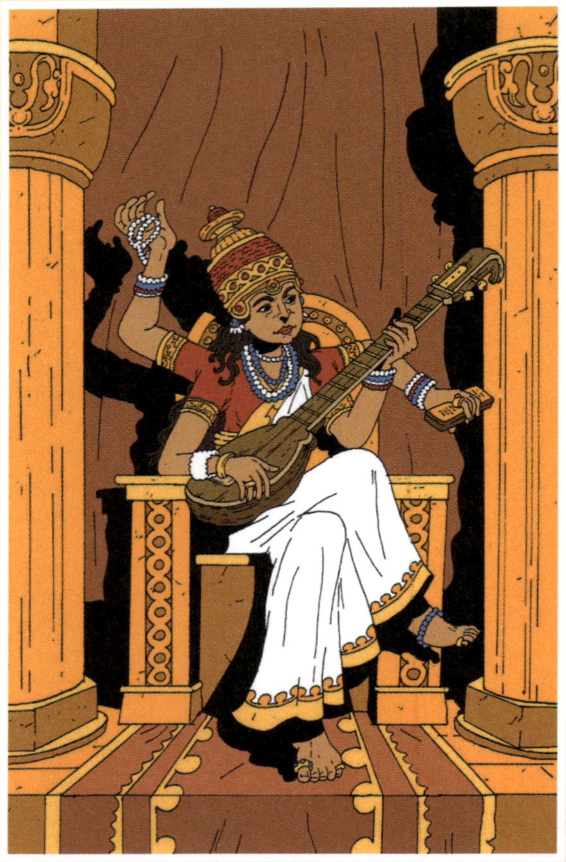

V - THE HIEROPHANT

SARASWATI

The Hierophant is a figure of mastery, a symbol of education, knowledge, and traditions that are transmitted in order to preserve the community as well as to elevate individuals and push them beyond the beaten path. Using a traditional itinerary, he introduces sacred things whose place and language he knows. In this deck, the Hierophant is represented by the Hindu goddess Saraswati, who, long before assuming her human semblance, was a river (one of the meanings of her name is "stream") that flowed down from the peaks of the Himalayas. What could better represent the flow of consciousness than a river? From a faraway spring in the mountains that tower over the world, it descends to the valley and into the towns where humans live, marking borders, rhythms, and seasons with its presence. The depiction of her seen here is the most classic: a wise woman carrying gifts in her four arms—devotion, music, and writing. She is the patron of arts and sciences, and she invented and offered the gift of Sanskrit, spoken and written language, to humankind. The most powerful learning tool, in fact, is writing. It has etched into the minds of many generations what has been, and it allows them to imagine what can be. Saraswati is eloquent and magnanimous: she suggests to her disciples, "Study your origins. Drink from the spring. It is the only way to change your future and redirect a course of events when it becomes necessary."

THE WITCH'S SPELLS

POSITIVE: education, faith, forgiveness, morality, guidance

NEGATIVE: obtuseness, bigotry, spiritual block, prejudice

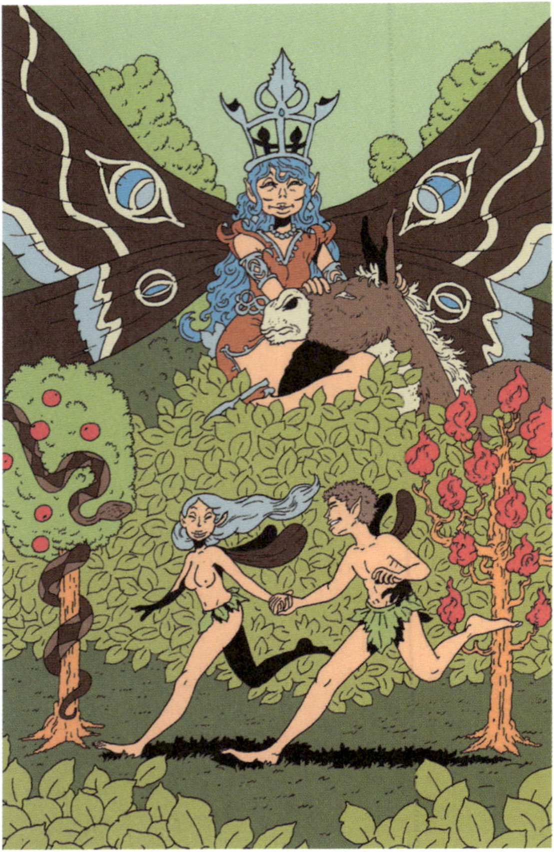

VI - THE LOVERS

TITANIA

According to widespread theology, during the darkest era, when they were being persecuted in the early modern ages in Europe and on the east coast of the United States, witches gained their evil powers by entering into pacts with the devil. But the confessions of some of them tell a different story. Many alleged witches did not know who the Christian devil was; they were more familiar with fairies—the arcane spirits of the fields, the woods, and the hills—and convened with the Queen of the Fairies in person to obtain their magic remedies. The most famous of the queens is Titania. Shakespeare conjured her in his comedy *A Midsummer Night's Dream*. She was beautiful and, after her husband Oberon ordered that a vengeful spell be cast on her, she fell in love with a man whose head was that of a donkey. Love, like fairies, is unpredictable and may even become obsession. The masses say it is blind, but those who have magic within say that it sees with other eyes, eyes that scrutinize the invisible, that hazy reign where fairies, elves, and restless spirits await us. Above all, love, with all its wonder, strangeness, and difficulties, is the ultimate step that leads us toward others and requires us to make choices. In the Land of Fairies, just as in the land of love, you can decide whether you want to blindly follow a selfish whim or whether you will use a truthful eye to recognize what is in front of you as you discover your most intimate part in another.

THE WITCH'S SPELLS

POSITIVE: love, choices, union, sexuality, romanticism

NEGATIVE: instability, sentimentalism, impulsiveness, frivolity

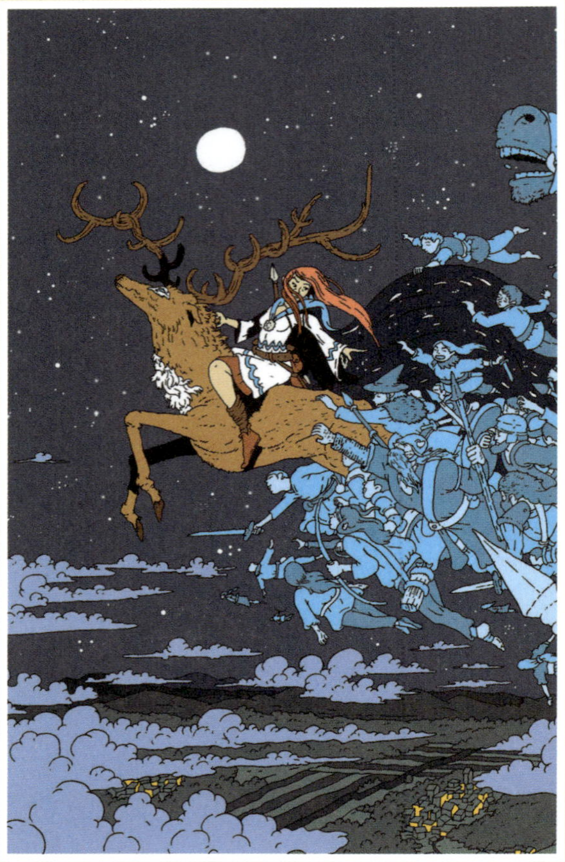

VII - THE CHARIOT

HOLDA

A woman rides across the night sky, leading a band of characters that at times shine like falling stars. If you look more closely, you can see animals and humans, and even children who hold on to the cape of Holda, the wild huntress of Germanic legends, and to the fur of the great stag of the forest, the symbol of spring, the season of rebirth. They are the spirits of the dead and of nature, moving across the earth in search of hospitality, some so they can return and some so they can abandon it forever. They trust in the benevolence of Holda, the goddess and witch who is daring and kind. When the end of the year draws near, the borders between worlds become fainter. The nights become magical, and you can feel the breath of those on the other side as they sigh. This depiction of the Chariot tempers the excessive ambition that sometimes characterizes it. With this card, we embark on a journey into the world to discover our true desire, the one that will never abandon us. When we depart, we establish what we wish to achieve, believing that nothing will hinder our progress but every voyage is a wandering filled with unexpected encounters. It will not be the destination but rather the path that shapes us, as it winds through things both material and spiritual. Holda leans down and extends her hand. It has the cold smell of the woods, of lost dreams and of flames that light up just on the other side of night. She says, "Do not leave anyone behind."

THE WITCH'S SPELLS

POSITIVE: ambition, travel, overcoming obstacles, positivity

NEGATIVE: yearning, unscrupulousness, lack of control, presumption

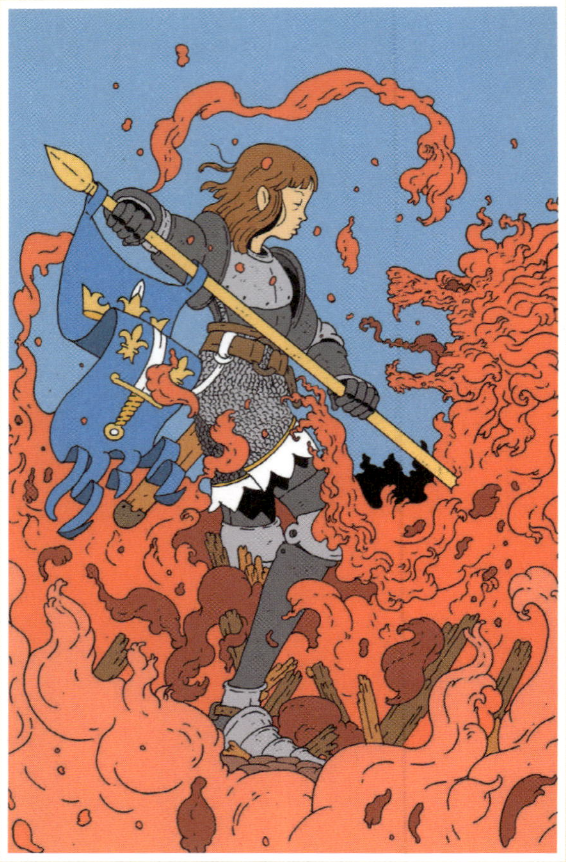

VIII - STRENGTH

JOAN OF ARC

Some people are born into great, harsh destinies that they will have to face with courage; but often, even to face common destinies, we must use our hidden resources and learn strength through resolute mildness. Joan of Arc, a warrior, a heretic, and a saint, encourages us to welcome the fire that destroys and purifies, just as you would with an indomitable soul. In the first half of the fifteenth century, an adolescent Joan took part in the Hundred Years' War to take back French lands that had fallen to the English. What could be expected of a small girl, driven by her faith and armed with only a banner and a sword? Yet her charisma was contagious, and captains admired her strength and her dedication. She wore her innocence like a transparent armor, which frightened the power-thirsty on one hand and roused the conscience of the people and of the soldiers on the other. Such ardor could not be defeated by death; it would shine on in a legend that would outlive her and continue to speak to the populations. The card of Strength is the will of the fire, the human and the lion who confront each other and become one another: sense and sensibility coming together to face difficulty. Defeat is not in losing the battle; it is in repressing fragility and a love that is selfless and sometimes naïve but strong, a love that makes utopias a reality in people and in places.

THE WITCH'S SPELLS

POSITIVE: strength, resistance, perseverance, courage, vitality

NEGATIVE: conceit, brutality, abuse of power, obstinacy

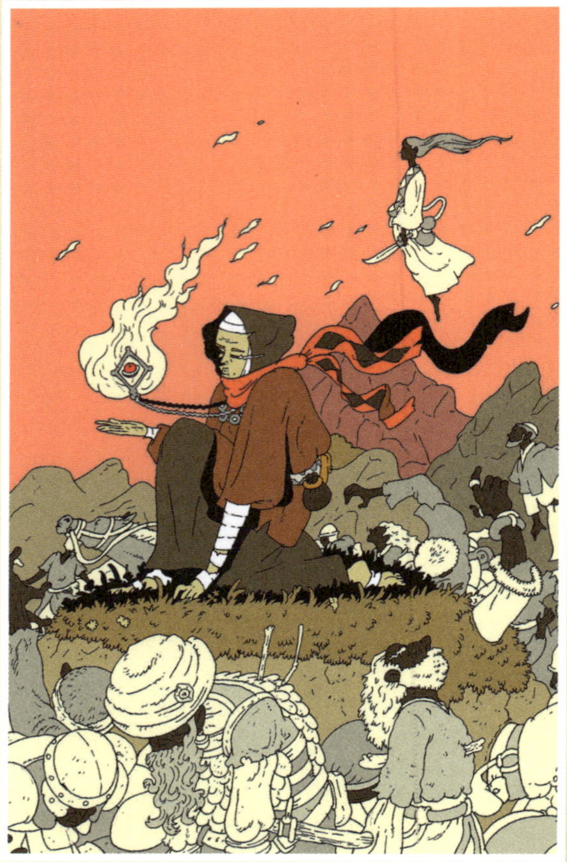

IX - THE HERMIT

THE WITCH OF ENDOR

In the Old Testament, Saul, the first king of Israel, prohibited all contact with magic and banished those who practiced the art; but when the outcome of the war against the Philistines became unclear, he dressed up as a vagabond to go visit the last remaining witch: a necromancer who lived in the city of Endor. Necromancy is the art of summoning the recently departed before they leave this world for the next, in order to take advantage of their wisdom. Saul requested that the woman summon the spirit of the prophet Samuel, who had just died, so that he could ask for his advice about the upcoming battle. The witch was understandably more afraid of the king and his laws than she was of the dead she summoned. Her art was bitter and solitary and is well suited to the card of the Hermit, a symbol of a personal path along which to pursue one's own knowledge, far from the fleeting goals of society. The Hermit's awareness takes dedication; he cares nothing about recognition. It comes from immersing himself in a room, a cave, or a corner that is all his. As a guide, the Hermit does not guarantee success, but rather teaches you to create unique instruments that will bring into focus your identity, your affinities, and those who accompany you in your adventures. The Hermit does not overcome the obstacle in his path; rather, he studies it and turns it into a torch that will light up the invisible.

THE WITCH'S SPELLS

POSITIVE: creative solitude, mysticism, introspection, the spiritual path

NEGATIVE: isolation, marginalization, fear of others

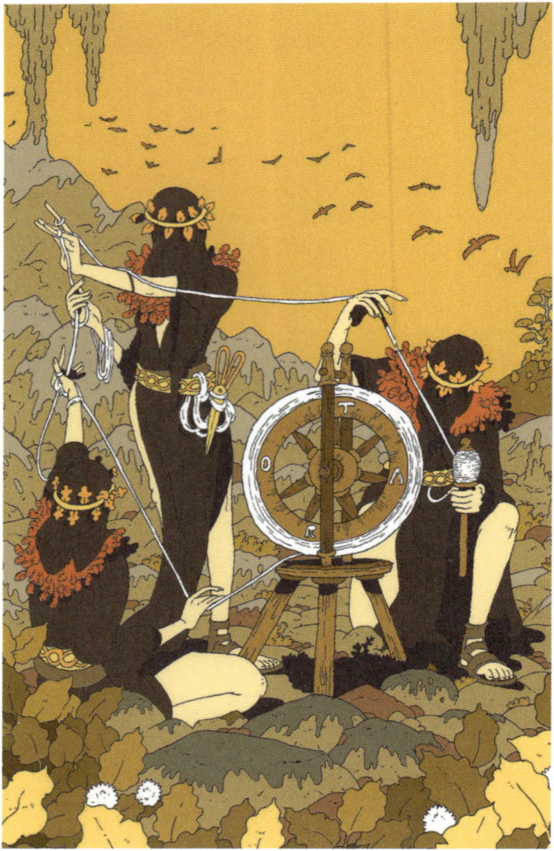

X - THE WHEEL OF FORTUNE

THE FATES

The Wheel of Fortune is probably one of the most suggestive and enigmatic of the cards. We can say that it is the essence of every Tarot reading—intuitive, divinatory, and meditative—since in it, fortunes revolve and destinies are revealed. It equally represents fated power in the hands of unknown forces and a game of fortune in which our choices play a fundamental role. In this deck, the Wheel is a spinning wheel where the three Fates—Clotho, Lachesis, and Atropos—worked incessantly from dawn until well after dusk, spinning, measuring, and cutting the thread of life. Their features are covered and we do not know which of the three faces will appear; we may believe that time is linear, but in reality it revolves with the spinning wheel and around the spindle, retracing cycles, faltering on knots and tears, and dreaming and remembering. The Wheel can instill fear, like the face of a stranger. Its movement may launch us into misfortune just as it may save us from the dark; or, worse, leave us hanging between the two. The work of the Fates is to neither punish nor reward, but their impartiality encourages us to become responsible in change. Everything is interconnected in the Wheel: ourselves, those beside us, and our collective fate. Beyond the veil, each of the Fates inevitably interrogates us in a whisper, as though from a black mirror: in the fleeting revolution of your days, look at your relationships and look after them.

THE WITCH'S SPELLS

<u>POSITIVE:</u> good luck, change, great works, overview

<u>NEGATIVE:</u> bad luck, mishaps, upset

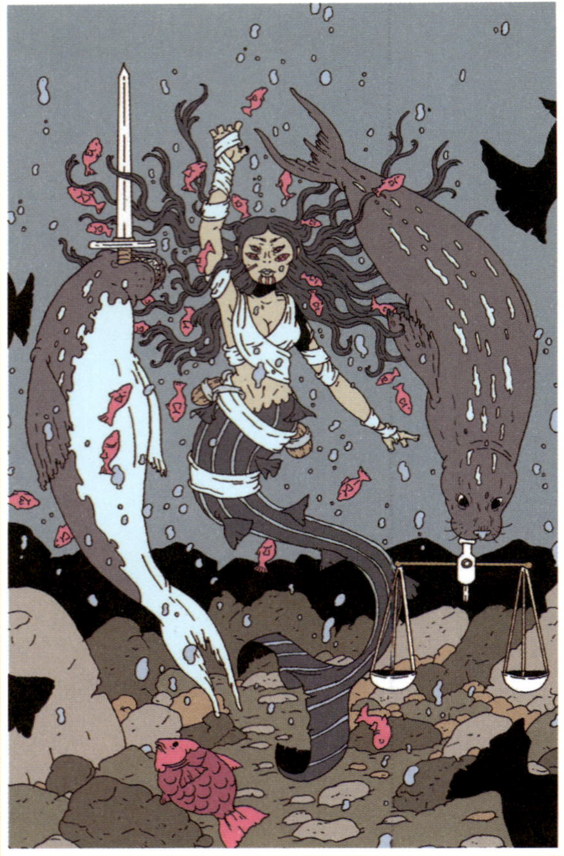

XI - JUSTICE

SEDNA

What is Justice, and how does it work? We know there is a system of justice, decreed by man in order to live together in society, and another greater justice that governs the cosmos. The concept is illustrated in a traditional short story from Inuit mythology that narrates how communal injustice affects the universal order. During a period of famine at the top of the world, in the Arctic, a community decided to embark on a journey in search of food. They built a raft and all of them got on; but when a small orphan named Sedna tried to join them, they pushed her away and she fell into the water. She tried to hold on to the sides of the raft, but the others cut off her fingers and left her to die; but she did not drown. Instead, her fingers turned into the world's first seals. The seals came to her rescue and carried her to the bottom of the sea, where she became the Mother of the Sea and the Lady of All Beasts, in the water and on land. From her oceanic home, she sees everything that humans do, and she punishes them when they violate life's unwritten rules, when they kill too many animals and destroy the planet, or when they are driven by greed and power. Sedna does not forget those who act without compassion, and she fills our souls with the fear of what we are capable of doing. She waits to weigh our hearts; and she reminds us that we are not the masters, and that every injustice we commit against others is a wound that we inflict on ourselves.

THE WITCH'S SPELLS

POSITIVE: retribution, truth, justice, cosmic law, impartiality

NEGATIVE: revenge, dishonesty, denial, corruption

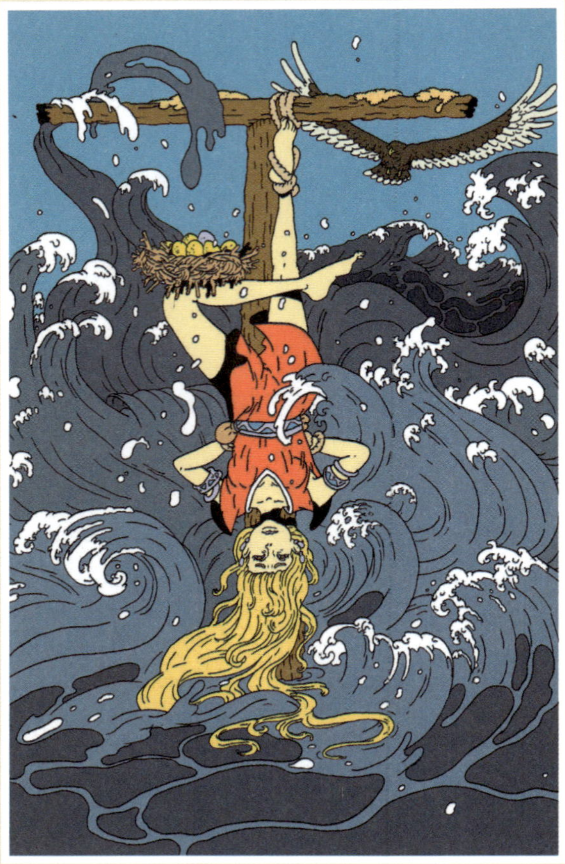

XII - THE HANGED MAN

LUONNOTAR

In Finnish mythology, the birth of the world is attributed to the virgin Luonnotar, a daughter of nature. When she grew tired of her lonely life in the sky, she came down to Earth and began to roam the seas. The waves and the wind impregnated her, and she carried the weight in her womb for . . . seven hundred years! As she floated, she saw a water bird looking for a place to nest, so she offered it her knee. The bird laid six eggs of gold and one of iron and began brooding them. Luonnotar was able to resist for three days, but the heat of the eggs burned like fire. When the eggs broke, they became the earth's surfaces, the heavenly bodies, and the clouds. Then Luonnotar gave shape to everything else—the coastline, the islands, and the abysses. When she gave birth to the poet Väinämöinen, he was already old but he was eager to gaze at the stars, the moon, and the sun, which he was finally able to see as it rose after years of wandering. Väinämöinen was the hero of the nineteenth century poem *Kalevala*, in which this story is told. The incredibly long wait characterizes the sacrificial choice of the Hanged Man, who cultivates his enormous potential hanging upside down. There are times when the only way to make sense of things is to look at them in reverse, choosing to observe rather than to act. It is in this way that we will be able to count the stars of the heavens after having long dreamed about them at the bottom of the sea.

THE WITCH'S SPELLS

POSITIVE: initiation, expectation, poetry, spiritual searching, selfless action

NEGATIVE: obstacles, suffering, indecision, waste, useless sacrifice

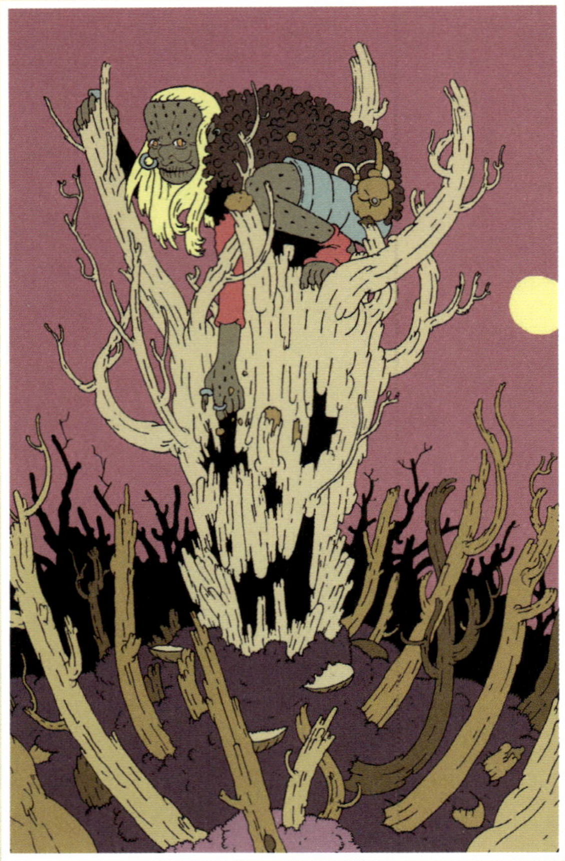

XIII - DEATH

BABA YAGA

Standing on chickens' legs, a restless house in the woods spins around, and, as it revolves, it alternately opens upon the world of the living and the world of the dead. The woman who lives there puts coals into the skulls that are on the gates so they can see who is coming. She is immortal and flies in a mortar and, with a pestle as her rudder, calls invisible servants to assist her. In Slavic folklore, Baba Yaga is a grandmother, a cannibal, and a counselor who tests legendary heroes. In her presence, vegetation turns bare and spectral, with no way to defend itself from her. Baba Yaga carries the lessons of the Dead and of their passing to another state of being (and therefore another birth), which requires sacrifice, surrender, and the acceptance of radical change. Baba Yaga scares us to our bones because she reminds us of the substance we are made of and of the wind whistling in skeletons. In order to stay alive, we must keep a firm hold on our dreams and let go of our life patterns and our useless beliefs. Perhaps Baba Yaga will devour us or hurt us as she chases us through the branches; but she will also tell us the truth about the mortal nature of experience. Listen as she caws in her beastly voice, "Take this chance, unburden yourself to the essence, and from the essence be reborn."

THE WITCH'S SPELLS

POSITIVE: transformation, passage, powerful movement, resolution, liberation

NEGATIVE: loss, separation, fear of change, perpetration of negative patterns

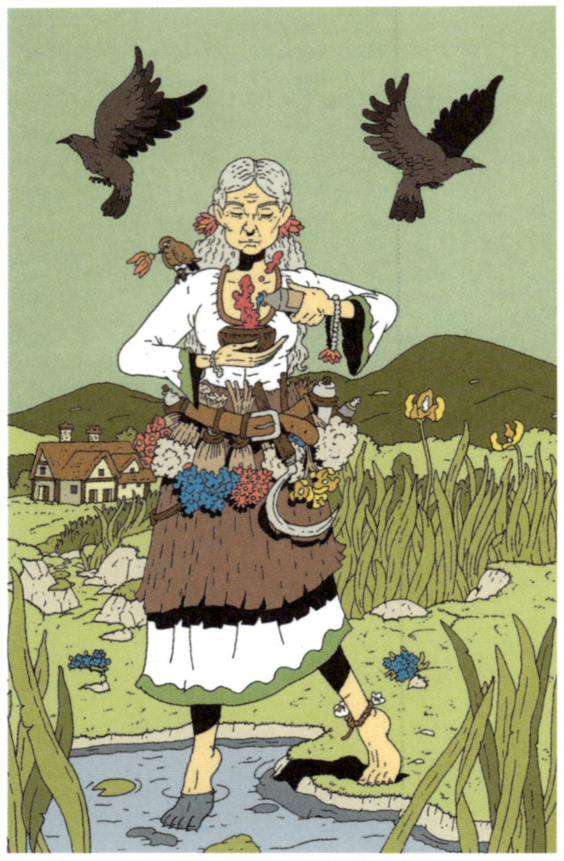

XIV - TEMPERANCE

BIDDY EARLY

We are at the height of the nineteenth century, and every morning Biddy Early leaves her Irish cottage to gather the medicinal herbs, the waters of the sacred spring, and the first dew, all of which will make the darkness light. She seals them in a Blue Bottle that was a gift from her dead son, who won it for her in a contest with the fairies. From the time she was a child, she has listened to the wisdom of the fairies, learning to probe daily occurrences with one eye as she observes the secrets of nature with the other. She mixes both into her potions, because any ingredient in the proper dose can be curative if it is tempered with patience. To wait is to see, be it the rising sun in the night or the seed of reconciliation with weakness in sickness. Biddy knows all this. She was an orphan. She faced the powerful and she worked hard as she cultivated her magic, but it never embittered her. A small, indomitable wren sits on her shoulder. When the Temperance card appears, it is a spirit that watches over us. Sometimes, when it comes to visit us, it looks at us with disillusion but without resignation to the many cracks in our existence. It comes to remind us that, at times, the most effective act is to not act at all. The first step of healing is to name that which afflicts us. Let the purification flow from the wound after our pain. Biddy reminds us that harmony within ourselves and others leads to beauty but is born in the shadows.

THE WITCH'S SPELLS

<u>POSITIVE</u>: temperance, patience, meeting of opposites, peace

<u>NEGATIVE</u>: extremism, impetuosity, rashness

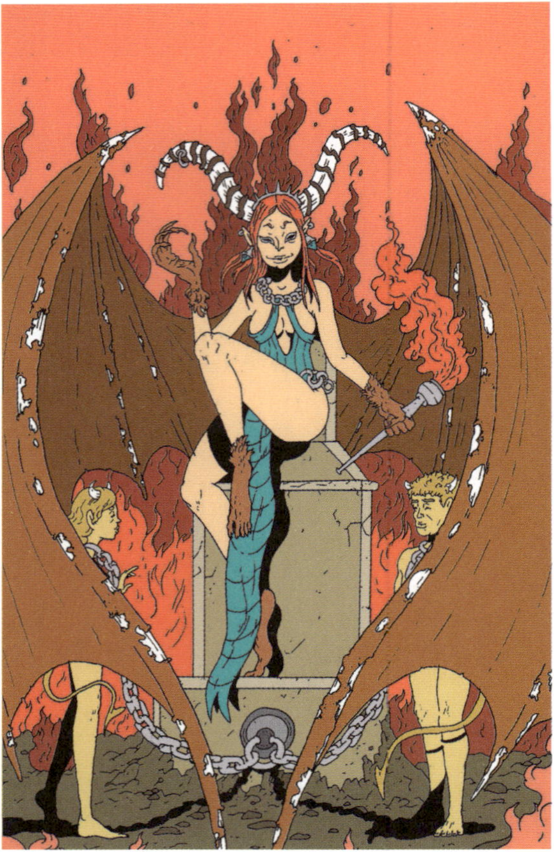

XV - THE DEVIL

LILITH

Many feel judged by the card of The Devil because of old stereotypes and old moral relics. Rules have been disobeyed, passion has led us to excess, and we are too much or too little for the society we attempt to live in. Really? Let's begin by saying that Tarot cards make no judgments and, if anything, they overturn them. Those who dare to face off with the Devil on equal terms will discover that behind the demon lies the principle of self-determination. They will discover the story of Lilith. Some Middle Eastern myths and some Jewish texts narrate that before Eve, Adam was married to Lilith. Her constitution was coarser than that of men, but she refused to be mentally or sexually submissive to her husband or to her role as a parent, so she was banished from the Garden of Eden. In some versions of the tale, she comes back to the garden as a snake and shares her knowledge with Eve; while in others, she continues to live in harmony with nature; and in yet others, she joins the company of various demons, never missing Paradise. She became a feminist icon over time that speaks to anyone looking for their own voice, regardless of gender. Sometimes we become toxically and destructively addicted to that which hurts us, only for lack of self-love. Other times we raise our heads and fly away, and it makes no difference if our wings are bat wings rather than angel's wings, because someone as free as ourselves will embrace us.

THE WITCH'S SPELLS

POSITIVE: sexuality, reclaiming one's own power, wildness, nonconformity

NEGATIVE: dependence, excess, subjugation, self-destruction

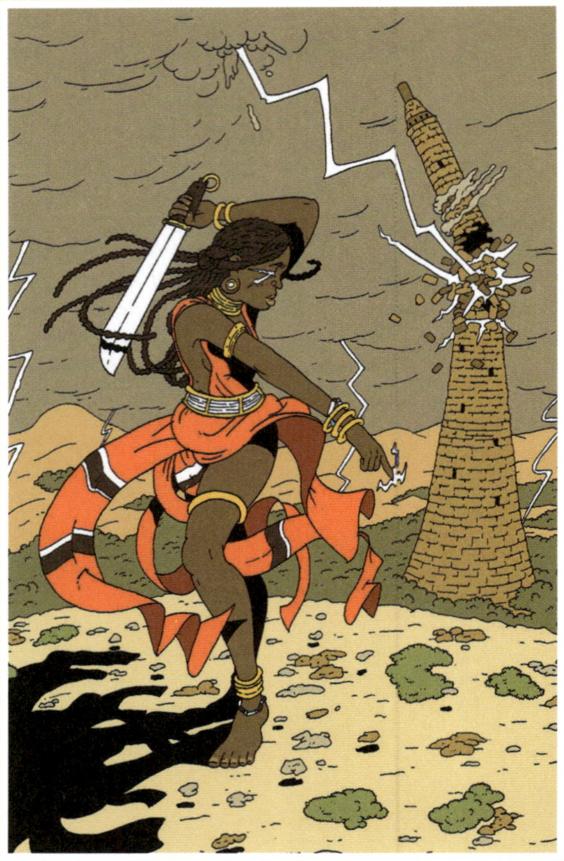

XVI - THE TOWER

OYA

The Tower crumbles and that which was once stable is no more, that which we built has not stood up to the test of time and events. Something within us has fallen and cannot get up again. The Tower is the symbol of ruin and desperation. Yet something has been freed, the walls that impeded our vision of the cosmos are gone, the beliefs that were consuming us are demolished. Oya is one of the Orisha, the godlike spirits or creatures in the folklore of the Yoruba people of Nigeria. Oya appears without warning, bad-tempered and ferocious like the wind. She commands tornadoes and floods and other natural disasters. She lights the fire of lightning bolts and knows how to wield a sword; she watches over cemeteries and can transform herself into the terrible Red Buffalo that makes the earth shake. But at times, destruction leads to regeneration, as her stories show us. Another Orisha, Osonyn, wanted to keep a squash full of medicinal plants all for herself, but Oya discovered that the squash was hidden at the top of a very tall tree. She unleashed winds that scattered the plants on the spirits that were under the tree, increasing the healing power of the herbs that could then be shared by everyone. Like the storm, the Tower disturbs nature, which is the only way that the life cycle can be renewed. At times it is much more damaging to resist change than to accept it.

THE WITCH'S SPELLS

POSITIVE: renewal, higher learning, liberation

NEGATIVE: collapse, devastation, crisis, danger, materialism

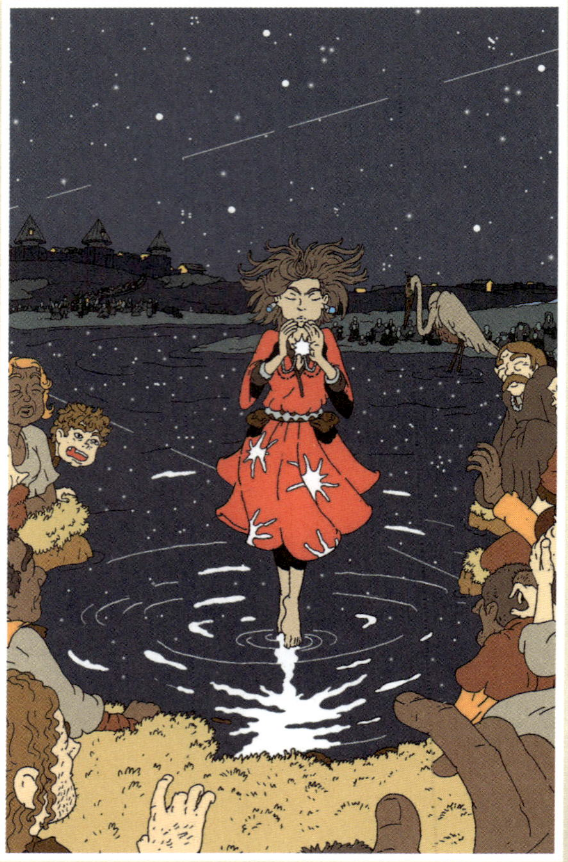

XVII - THE STAR

ARADIA

After a long journey, a heron returns to its home waters, bearing messages from the living—their hopes. He entrusts them to the waters that reflect the quiet night and the stars. One star sees them and comes to the water's edge, where it lands on its toes as if it were dancing. It is Aradia, the daughter of Diana, the Queen of the Witches and creator of the rain, the stars, and the sky that surrounds them. According to modern legend, she brought witchcraft not only to the oppressed and defeated, the victims persecuted by the powerful, but also to every individual who felt out of place and repressed as well. What exactly is the art of witchcraft? So much more than potions and rituals, it is the poetic force of the imagination, the ability to perceive bridges and pathways where most see only abysses and barriers and to walk into the future without ignoring the facts of the present. It is the hope that restores your soul, that opens your eyes to a landscape of possibilities, and that asks, above all, that you do not surrender. With the patience of the water that wears away the rock or of the memory of who we are and who we can become, a memory that gives dignity to all suffering, Aradia takes the heron's messages and sends him back into the world. When the Star appears, it asks us to shine, to listen to its promises. Regardless of what happens, we are part of life and we give light to a star, the Star that is all of us.

THE WITCH'S SPELLS

<u>POSITIVE:</u> hope, inspiration, faith, healing, spirituality

<u>NEGATIVE:</u> desperation, mistrust, discomfort

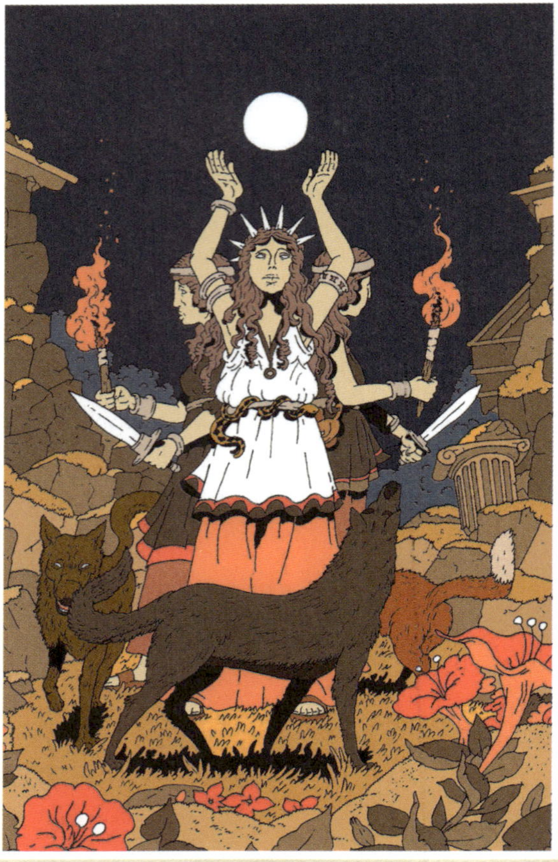

XVIII - THE MOON

HECATE

In Greek mythology, Hecate is a triadic deity who, when we reach a crossroads, shows us the way between the pathways of hopes and anxieties and between the material and the spiritual. Just like her faithful companions, she barks at the moon, whether it be full, a crescent, or new. Hecate shines her torch on the world of the living and the worlds beyond, where wild beings, the dead, and faraway divinities exist. They feast in the light of the moon on the offerings left by humans. For an instant, they form a circle and every illusion becomes reality; all that is commonplace becomes disturbing, grotesque, and mysterious, like in a night dream. It must be remembered that Hecate is the patron of witches, an ancient goddess whose origins are pre-Indo-European and who speaks the language of the dead. She oversees childbirth and newborns just as she oversees the universes that have yet to come into existence and truths that can be perceived from afar. Some prophetic dreams belong to her, just as they belong to the Moon card, who overwhelms us with strange apparitions when we begin to search within ourselves for clarity, the lasting wonder in a forest of deceptions. To call upon Hecate or the Moon is to embark on a pathway into our dead zones, the ones that frighten us; it is to dress up as a ghost who awaits in the shadows. There, we forge our magic words and make our return, like the star that grows larger after it disappears.

THE WITCH'S SPELLS

POSITIVE: dreams, intuition, untamed world, clairvoyance, subconscious

NEGATIVE: deceit, anxiety, neurosis, fear, incomprehension

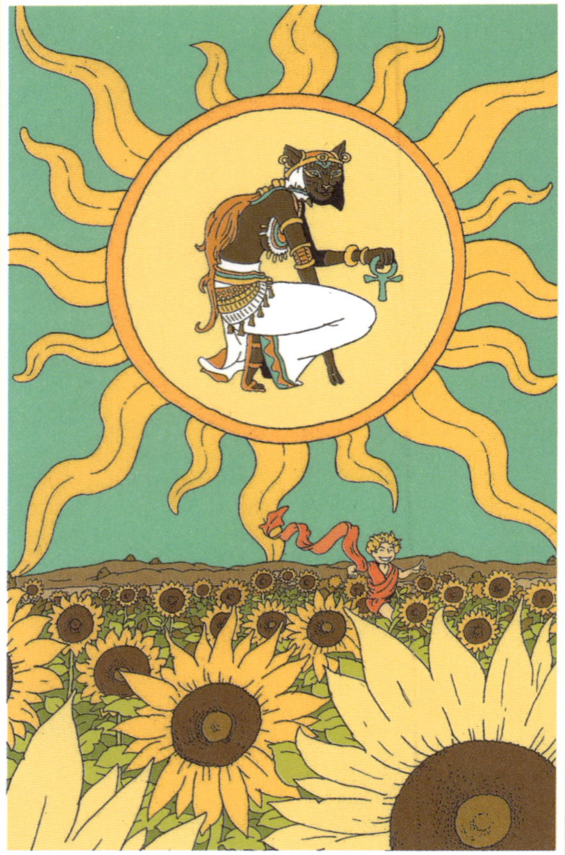

XIX - THE SUN

BASTET

The cat stirs in its bed, dreaming about a time when it lived in the Valley of the Nile as a goddess, adored by the population, both as a human and as a feline. Her race was highly esteemed; they hunted mice to protect the harvested wheat that was the color of gold and of the day. Her name was Bastet. Is Bastet. She brings warmth, love, and joyous feasts. She is the goddess of dance and seduction. Beauty attracts beauty. Whoever embraces Bastet embraces health and a bit of her astute feline witchcraft and, with it, learns to enjoy every favorable occasion and every corner of the world that the sun warms with its light. She protects the home and its secrets, but she also has a predatory, aggressive side that allows her to do merciless battle with her enemies. The nineteenth card illuminates every existence, granting self-awareness and the results it can bring. The card is so dazzling that it is almost impossible to look at it; we have to close our eyes and let it draw near our bodies, brightening them as it does. Whenever this card appears, it takes us back to the child that laughs within us, to the innocence of an animal who needs little to be happy: food, rest, and love. The essentials. The cat stretches as she dreams. She smiles with an almost-human expression that immediately vanishes into ineffable joy as she runs. In the Sun.

THE WITCH'S SPELLS

POSITIVE: well-being, lasting success, health, vitality

NEGATIVE: impossible expectations, unhappiness

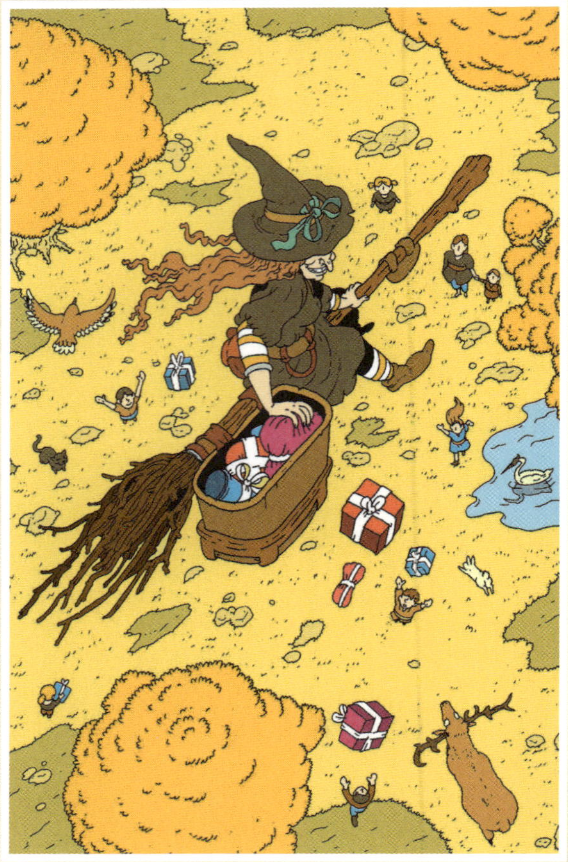

XX - JUDGMENT

BEFANA

During the first nights of the New Year, an old witch flies in the skies. Her clothes are simple, she rides a traditional broom, and she knows how to navigate using the stars. In ancient folklore, she is the symbol of the year gone by and the keeper of the harvest that is to come. In the most common tradition, she brings gifts for the children and brings back the capacity for childlike wonder to the adults. She is called Befana. She is both cantankerous and benevolent, much more so than the other famous bearers of gifts that populate traditions. Befana fills our stockings with all that is sweet and bitter in our past experiences, teaching us that a new start is a new approach to our center and to our essence. According to Christian tradition, Befana showed the Three Wise Men the way to the stable of the Christ Child. They invited her to join them, but she arrived late and found neither the Wise Men nor the Holy Infant. That was the beginning of her winter adventure, bringing gifts to children in the hopes that one of them would be Jesus and she could ask for his pardon. Perhaps she forgot her search as she began to delight in what she was doing. There is a divine infant in each of us, and in every life there is dignity. Befana comes down from the sky to remind us of our expectations for what is good. In the Judgment card, we find our vocation and we forgive the past. Our memory grows light, and if we cry it is tears of joy. Every gift is a reconciliation.

THE WITCH'S SPELLS

POSITIVE: vocation, acceptance, forgiveness, liberation

NEGATIVE: unawareness, self-deprecation

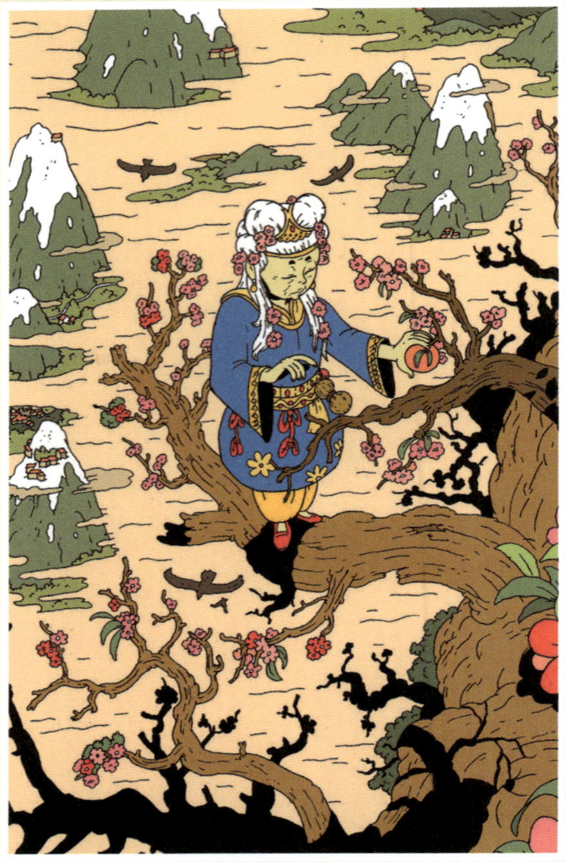

XXI - THE WORLD

XIWANGMU

Here we are, before the world, our own world as our shelter and the great world in which to lose our selves and live our adventures. From the peaks of the Kunlun Mountains, Xiwangmu, the Queen Mother of the West in Chinese legend, knows that the trip is a long one and that it crosses the borders of time and space. It is the measure of the soul, where height and depth meet and where an instant is equal to centuries of study. She may await the traveler in her cave, or she may come out to her garden in the clouds, where the cosmic tree that connects the heavens to the earth grows. Every three thousand years, the peaches of maturity ripen on its branches. Xiwangmu has changed her shape. Once she had the tail of a leopard and the teeth of a tiger. She brought pestilence to humankind, but she is also a healer and a protector. She is an ancestor, the grandmother of all, as old as the cosmos whose health and diseases she carries within. To reach her is to embrace the World and become immortal. But what does that mean exactly? Maybe the secret that the Queen Mother of the West holds is being given back to the World, to feel that everything flows from within to without, as though every accomplishment is the contemplation of the beginning. In the mountains of the West, as we eat a piece of fruit, we open our eyes. This is where we have always been. At home.

THE WITCH'S SPELLS

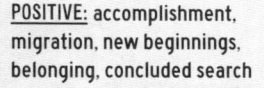

POSITIVE: accomplishment, migration, new beginnings, belonging, concluded search

NEGATIVE: incompleteness, emptiness, failure

SYMBOLS OF THE MINOR ARCANA

ACE OF WANDS

The Ace of Wands is the magic wand that links the witch to the wisdom of the wood, the leaves, the fire, and the ashes that fertilize the ground after destruction. The wand evokes all the characters of a story and, above all, instinctively knows what path to take and in which vision to immerse oneself. It creates a door of the wood that it is made of, and opens it onto all that can be created.

THE WITCH'S SPELLS

POSITIVE: creation, vital spark, instinct, imagination

NEGATIVE: lack of energy, lack of goals

TWO OF WANDS

A miniature world floats in the palm of the witch of the Two of Wands. A scene filled with encounters and places to explore opens before her. If the imagined world is to become real, there must be careful planning; knowledge and outside air must be allowed to filter into the intellect, to limit impulsive action, and to guide enthusiasm in the right direction. This card signifies departure and asks us to bring our dreams down to earth, step by step.

THE WITCH'S SPELLS

POSITIVE: planning, departure, important decisions

NEGATIVE: fear of change, hastily made plans

THREE OF WANDS

The witch of the Three of Wands gazes into the distance at the last remaining ship on the horizon. To see, she uses her mortal eyes and those of her second sight, which perceive the invisible. It is impossible to describe her vision with simple words, without using art, magic, and poetry. What she sees is the dance of fate as it shifts between deep waters, storms, and sunny banks. In the sails, she is able to hear lives that are yet to come, the most extraordinary of adventures.

THE WITCH'S SPELLS

POSITIVE: vision, premonition, adventure, travel to foreign lands

NEGATIVE: frustration, delay, disappointed expectations

FOUR OF WANDS

Surrounded by the lushness of spring, two witches wave with bouquets of flowers from a stairway that leads to the city. Behind them, a circle of dancing people can be seen. The day is a happy one, a celebration of obtained results and of the beginning of a new path, a communal feast, a personal tradition, and a moment in which we retire to our own spaces to regenerate. In the Four of Wands, we experience a moment for ourselves and for those we love. We celebrate being together on the unpredictable path of life.

THE WITCH'S SPELLS

<u>POSITIVE:</u> celebration, festivity, roots

<u>NEGATIVE:</u> family conflicts, lack of support

FIVE OF WANDS

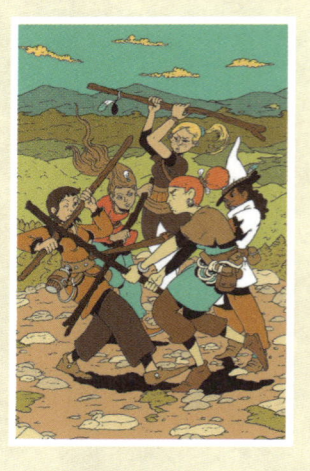

In the Five of Wands, a group of witches challenges one another in a battle that is both playful and contentious—a personal conflict, perhaps. Each of them is convinced she is right and wants her voice to be heard; but as all of them shout, they are deaf to the words of the others. Perhaps they will sit down in the evening, forgetting the cause of their discord, or they may choose to put down their wands and opt for a more mature form of confrontation. The energy that comes from unity is abundant, just as the energy wasted for the whims of the ego is.

THE WITCH'S SPELLS

POSITIVE: truce, reaching agreement, end of conflict

NEGATIVE: fighting, tension, competition

SIX OF WANDS

The cheers that greet the witch of the Six of Wands as she comes into the village with her head held high do not make her feel arrogant or disdainful. Her horse is festively decorated, but she is wearing her daily garb. We often look for recognition of our talents in the wrong place, and many times we have to move on to find appreciation. Humility and triumph ride together in this card. Only when we have won the battle against our own insecurities can we fight against the prejudice of others.

THE WITCH'S SPELLS

POSITIVE: public success, a happy return, compensation

NEGATIVE: lack of recognition, private results, egotism

SEVEN OF WANDS

The witch defends her space from others who are closing in, armed to overtake her. In the Seven of Wands, the witch is a voice that stands out from the crowd, unafraid of demonstrating her diversity. The fear of losing what she has sparks the beginnings of fierceness; she must be able to protect the freedom she has gained. She knows that the most difficult battle is not the one fought to achieve a goal, but the one fought to hold on to it. She is ready to fight.

THE WITCH'S SPELLS

POSITIVE: defense, uniqueness, self-assertion

NEGATIVE: lack of self-confidence, submissiveness

EIGHT OF WANDS

Eight wands slice through the air, aimed with certitude toward their target. In the Eight of Wands, opportunity is there for the taking and we are full of enthusiasm, strength, and determination. Every message we receive becomes a solution or a new project. Everything hinges on action and, in fact, the absence of humans is conspicuous. The general meaning of the card is movement, which can signify a desired journey, a productive meeting, or an expected change of direction.

THE WITCH'S SPELLS

POSITIVE: change, excitement, travel, dynamism

NEGATIVE: delays, missing of chances, unpreparedness

NINE OF WANDS

The witch has been walking a long time looking for herbs and fruit for her spells and for her nourishment. She is tired. Seeing humans losing respect for nature and ransacking it at will has made her weary of her wanderings in the world; she feels that her spirit has been ransacked as well. In the Nine of Wands, she goes back to her valley near the stream and finds comfort in her old feline companion. She is ready to defend the beauty of her spaces.

THE WITCH'S SPELLS

POSITIVE: resilience, daily courage, the will to take sides

NEGATIVE: fatigue, lack of motivation

TEN OF WANDS

A witch carrying a heavy load struggles up the road. She is nearing the village, but this last effort could be too much for her. When we arrive at the Ten of Wands, we have already seen a lot of conflict about ideas, dignity, and survival, and we are unable to carry any more weight. If we take on other burdens, they will not make us happier; they will only make us wearier. So now we must choose what is essential and retire to the threshold of rest and relief.

THE WITCH'S SPELLS

POSITIVE: responsibility, duty, daily struggle

NEGATIVE: oppressive burden, exhaustion, inability to delegate

PAGE OF WANDS

New leaves sprout from the witch's wand; they symbolize enthusiastic expectations for the future in a landscape that has yet to bear its fruit. Behind her is a hare, an indomitable spirit in the body of the small herbivore who signals the arrival of spring. The Page of Wands embodies the curious nature of children and their desire to dive into the world and animate it with their ideas. Where others see nothing, he sees infinite possibilities. Do not let your imagination run away with you; focus your attention on his many projects and challenges.

THE WITCH'S SPELLS

POSITIVE: adventure, a congenial spirit, cheer, fresh ideas

NEGATIVE: infantilism, impatience, distraction

KNIGHT OF WANDS

The wild goose of the Knight of Wands is preparing to take flight, perhaps leading a flock on its way to a warm place for the winter. The goose and the witch inspire crowds and never seem to lose their way, and, should they get lost, their curiosity and their spirit of adaptation will enable them to navigate unfamiliar skies. The Knight is a fascinating guide who is unafraid of confrontation and does not tolerate defeat. His dreams for himself and for others are big and sometimes his energy is bigger than reality, making the consequences of his actions unpredictable.

THE WITCH'S SPELLS

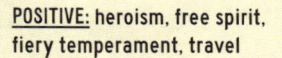

POSITIVE: heroism, free spirit, fiery temperament, travel

NEGATIVE: arrogance, inconsistency, unpredictability

QUEEN OF WANDS

Witch, shaman, friend of the fairies and of the hidden people, healer and caster of spells, we have before us the Queen of Wands—the lady of sorcery, dispenser of herbal knowledge, generous, absorbed by her world but quite able to carry on the most banal of conversations with brilliance. Willful, extravagant, and unpredictable, one moment she is present, and the next she is off to mysterious destinations to avoid her boredom with common mortals. She may be a bit too egocentric, but she is always willing to come to the aid of the most fragile. After all, she is the one with magic mushrooms who sees through the eyes of cats.

THE WITCH'S SPELLS

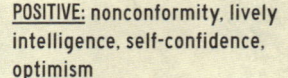

POSITIVE: nonconformity, lively intelligence, self-confidence, optimism

NEGATIVE: vengefulness, egoism, arrogance, intrusiveness

KING OF WANDS

The lynx is the most mysterious of woodland animals, and to meet one is an event! With an extremely acute sense of both sight and smell, it perceives the reality behind the façade. As it accompanies the King of Wands, the lynx embodies the element of fire and adds the decisiveness of the charismatic leader to the brilliance of the other face cards in the suit. In fact, the King, like the lynx, reflects and sharpens his senses in order to fulfill his visions. The fire generated by the King destroys to create. It consumes old hides, seasons, and lives already lived, in which we linger uselessly, and ushers in a new world.

THE WITCH'S SPELLS

<u>POSITIVE:</u> leadership, taking control, initiative, courageous decisions, sharp sense of vision

<u>NEGATIVE:</u> inefficiency, weak leadership, brutality

ACE OF CUPS

The witch looks at herself in the water collected in the Ace of Cups. She recognizes the lives of those she has loved: humans, animals, plants, and beings from her dreams. She takes a sip in order to remember. The water is cool, pungent, bitter, sad, and moving. It is feeling in all of its facets, none of which can be neglected. Then she pours the contents into the river so that water can reconnect with water. Those who love let go when the time comes and welcome the water of their tears as the water of joy.

THE WITCH'S SPELLS

POSITIVE: empathy, affection, new relationships, contemplation

NEGATIVE: emotional vacuum, loss of affection, narcissism

TWO OF CUPS

Strong ties are formed in the Two of Cups, where two figures meet and share a feeling. The nocturnal wisdom of the owl descends into their cups like blood, the liquid that holds the soul and gives life to the body. It takes the shape of Hermes's staff, indicating unity and conciliation between opposites. What happens in this card may last a moment in the world outside, but it will intimately affect the players. The meeting may be one of love, of friendship, or of mutual recognition of spiritual affinity.

THE WITCH'S SPELLS

<u>POSITIVE:</u> attraction, connection, unity of forces, mutual affection

<u>NEGATIVE:</u> separation, discord, breach

THREE OF CUPS

Three sisters, ancestresses and companions in adventure, a child, a mother, and an old woman, raise their chalices to fulfillment and joy. Harmony and fellowship emanate from this card as daily magic takes place: learning to live with others, giving dignity and a voice to each. The Three of Cups reminds us of the importance of family and community ties and of the trust we place in one another to expand the power of dreams and willpower in our relationships.

THE WITCH'S SPELLS

POSITIVE: sharing, joy, community, new social system

NEGATIVE: isolation, lack of empathy, frustrating relationships, diffidence

FOUR OF CUPS

A cup is offered to the witch of the Four of Cups, but she seems reluctant to take it. Perhaps she has been hurt and is afraid to open herself up to feelings and opportunities again. She sits, apathetic and refusing to choose. She must remember that she is choosing for herself, that a change for the better is not far away, and that one bitter cup does not make all cups bitter. Now is the time to take her attention away from her thoughts and look at the hand that is reaching out to her. Accept it.

THE WITCH'S SPELLS

POSITIVE: contemplation, acceptance, choosing to be happy

NEGATIVE: dissatisfaction, loss of goals, apathy, disconnection

FIVE OF CUPS

Though she may be wrapped in a cape of feathers, the witch cannot fly. She is weighed down by the pain of something she has lost, taken from her by the tide. The Five of Cups is a sad card. With desperation, the eyes and the mind contemplate that which has been. But nocturnal flowers are blooming, two of the cups are still whole, and life reclaims its part. The witch knows that she must cry all of her tears before she turns and gathers what remains.

THE WITCH'S SPELLS

POSITIVE: acceptance, knowing how to be satisfied, finding peace

NEGATIVE: loss, grief, inability to look ahead, sadness

SIX OF CUPS

A small boy offers a cup full of blue flowers to a little girl, the same flowers that fill the other five cups placed on the walls outside the house. They are forget-me-nots. With the flowers, the two characters give one another the gift of childhood and its dreams, its experiences, and even its pains. Every now and then it is good to go back to our early life, for comfort and to strengthen the roots of our affection. In the Six of Cups, the memory of who we were appears, a memory we must promise we will never forget.

THE WITCH'S SPELLS

POSITIVE: childhood, memories, family, comfort

NEGATIVE: inability to escape the past, sentimentalism, abandoning the home

SEVEN OF CUPS

The suit of cups represents our feelings, and this card asks us to evaluate the fantasies that derive from those feelings and to consider how possible it would be for them to become reality. The Seven of Cups deals with illusions and time spent fantasizing about impossible dreams, like riding a dragon, which of course is almost impossible because the wildest dragon in our imagination is only waiting for us to show him how to create shared universes.

THE WITCH'S SPELLS

POSITIVE: daydreaming, searching for a new purpose, making choices, opportunity, fantasies

NEGATIVE: illusions, lack of purpose, confusion

EIGHT OF CUPS

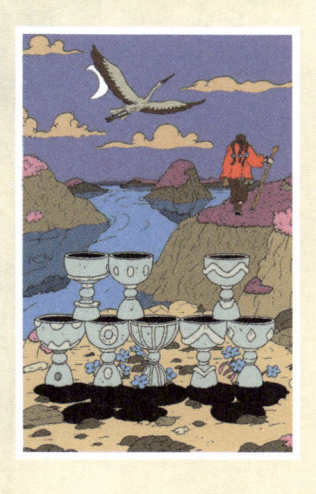

It is time to leave. The heron points the witch in the direction of her heart because the voice of the Eight of Cups is the heart. It asks us to embark on a journey, so we do not lose our dreams, and we must listen to it, even if we like the place we are in and we have learned to love its inhabitants. We have no idea of what the trip has in store for us and we have often regretted leaving our security behind, but our true home is the one we carry within us. Every separation prepares us for our return.

THE WITCH'S SPELLS

POSITIVE: disillusionment, journey, necessary travel, leaving something behind

NEGATIVE: fear of loss, avoidance of change

NINE OF CUPS

The witch that sits in the Nine of Cups is at the end of an emotional journey. The cups of her wishes granted can be seen behind her. She has learned to love herself and to share. Perhaps she is waiting for guests so she can celebrate with them. This card embodies a journey of sentiments that have ripened and are ready to overflow, just like the water in the cup, into something new. Her face shows some worry. On their negative side, feelings are vices in which we risk closing ourselves or losing ourselves.

THE WITCH'S SPELLS

POSITIVE: satisfaction, fulfilled wishes, happy love, gratitude

NEGATIVE: indulgence, vice, presumption, failure

TEN OF CUPS

The rainbow arches across the sky with its ten cups of joy. It reminds us of a secret pact between beings: make yourself happy, forgive yourself, and recognize the wonder of love. Love may last only as long as the colored arch in the sky, but it is a feeling that blesses the heart, and that blessing is a protection in times of difficulty. The people we see here are supporting one another emotionally after having survived a hurricane. They will survive more hurricanes in the future because they have found their true home, in each other's hearts and in their own.

THE WITCH'S SPELLS

POSITIVE: happy love, blessings, family unity, wonder

NEGATIVE: unhappy family, discord, emotional conflict

PAGE OF CUPS

The witch in the Page of Cups is depicted as a sensitive, colorful dreamer. Her soul is represented by her loud clothing. She wears her inside on her outside, and her sentimentality is her armor. The Pages symbolize the beginning of a path, and the path of this Page begins in the purity of emotions and in intuitively understood truths. The starfish, a symbol of sensitivity and healing, is a reminder that we can regenerate ourselves in our dreams, rediscovering our inner child, when all other pathways seem impassable. The Page of Cups teaches us that our emotions do not make us vulnerable; instead, they allow us to open ourselves to trust and inspire it in others.

THE WITCH'S SPELLS

POSITIVE: dreaming spirit, heart of a child, inner child

NEGATIVE: vulnerability, insecurity, escapism

KNIGHT OF CUPS

Having fished for fish and visions, the witch rides her heron upward into the sky. The Knight of Cups does not fear being accused of his lack of realism; he is bolstered by his desire for a life lived to the fullest, both emotionally and spiritually. The witch holds up her cup as a tribute to dreaming and to the importance of searching for something noble that will give purpose to her voyage. Idealist, kind, committed to actions that others deem impossible, she is convinced that faith and free spirit can penetrate stone like the beak of a bird piercing the clouds in the sky.

THE WITCH'S SPELLS

POSITIVE: idealism, goodness, following the path of the heart, artistic gifts

NEGATIVE: vanity, capriciousness, cowardice

QUEEN OF CUPS

Cetaceans are thought to possess extraordinary emotional intelligence. Humpback whales come to the aid of other animals, protecting them from killer whales. The back of a humpback whale forms an island on which the Queen of Cups sits barefoot, suggesting her contact with the profound. She is quiet, maternal, and kind. This witch is a healer who uses her empathy to help those in trouble and reminds us that only those who can mindfully love themselves can rise above and reach out to those around them. Her realm, as vast as the ocean, is in her heart.

THE WITCH'S SPELLS

POSITIVE: compassion, healing, spiritual guidance, kindness, support

NEGATIVE: fragility, martyrdom, excessive giving

KING OF CUPS

The King of Cups strides through a spring made of a river, shaking off a salmon. According to Celtic druids, after a mythological salmon swallowed a magic nut, anyone who ate at least a small piece of salmon would be granted his knowledge of worldly things. Water drips onto the witch's red hair from a cup of power as the water rises around her. What knowledge is she hiding? She has learned to listen to her instincts rather than repressing them. From them she draws the ability to judge, a knowledge that is quiet and constant and is never imposing.

THE WITCH'S SPELLS

POSITIVE: heart/mind balance, overcoming conflict, self-control

NEGATIVE: manipulation, anxiety, repression, emotional blackmail

ACE OF SWORDS

The witch wields her purifying blade in the Ace of Swords. She is ready to cut away the superfluous and move the winds so that they bring a storm to heal the scorched earth. The sword is the witch's voice and her intellect. She uses it to dialogue with others and convince them of her worthy cause. When the sword has excised the useless and the illusions, new radical perspectives with which to view the world can shine again.

THE WITCH'S SPELLS

POSITIVE: mental clarity, intellect, communication, concentration, truth

NEGATIVE: coercion, destruction, brute strength, lack of intellect

TWO OF SWORDS

At times, the noise of the world creates such confusion that it is impossible to make clear choices or to ponder and decide. The witch retires in isolation to her interior space, descending into the depths of her being. The two swords are the same, both with the same shining blades. Her guardian is the moon that lights up her mental processes. When it seems that both choices are equal, we have to consider the two with eyes other than our physical eyes, to recognize the enigma of the Two of Swords, and make room in ourselves for intuition and reason to meet.

THE WITCH'S SPELLS

POSITIVE: mental space, difficult decision, inner truth

NEGATIVE: indecision, stagnation, concealment

THREE OF SWORDS

The witch of the Three of Swords shows her pain. As she holds it in her hands, in a heart that is whole, even if it has been damaged, she looks away to avoid devastation. It is certainly true that, as many say, pain is a great test; but as we are experiencing it, we can do nothing except to feel it and to let it pour out of us with no regard for the judgment of others. Before we can face a test, we must accept it. This is particularly true for those tests that cause us pain.

THE WITCH'S SPELLS

POSITIVE: forgiveness, moving on, test

NEGATIVE: broken heart, pain, trauma, alienation

FOUR OF SWORDS

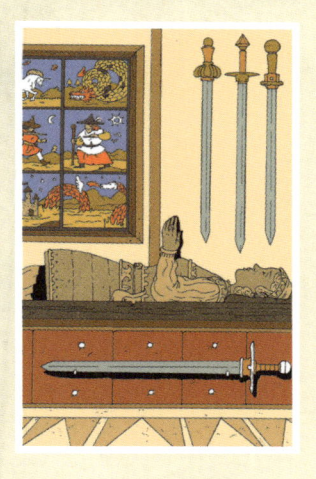

The witch of the Four of Swords lies so still that she looks like a statue. She is in her sanctuary, the space where she goes to restore her strength after a period of fatigue. The drawings on her windowpanes depict her past efforts. They have indubitably enriched her; but now that she can finally rest, weariness overcomes her. Taking a pause is healthy, and so is sleeping and spending your day with nothing to do in particular. Recreate empty space where your imagination can plant its seed.

THE WITCH'S SPELLS

POSITIVE: recovery of energy, rest, self-care, sanctuary

NEGATIVE: exhaustion, return to the world, restlessness

FIVE OF SWORDS

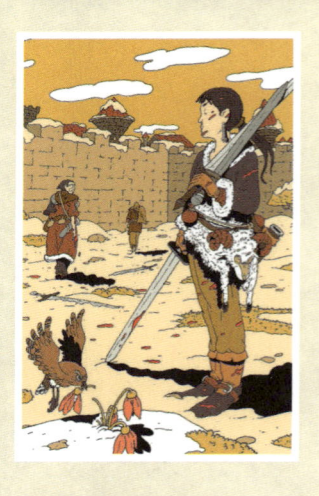

It is a battlefield where a warrior witch takes the arms of her enemies as other witches are lying on the ground and still others retreat. The Five of Swords depicts a ferocious battle from which both winner and loser will emerge embittered. A middle passage in life requires us to move toward clarification in ourselves and with others. A wren that picks a flower and takes it out of the debris is both a warning and a reminder; every defeat can lead to renewal.

THE WITCH'S SPELLS

POSITIVE: remorse, reconciliation, revenge, victory at a great price

NEGATIVE: hostility, defeat, abuse of power, fight, aggressiveness

SIX OF SWORDS

Flames float on the water, the lights of departure. On a simple boat, a witch-helmsman is escorting a woman and a child. The figures in the Six of Swords have their backs to us as they leave the life they know for another, full of promise. Sometimes we must put ourselves into the hands of others because, alone, we are unable to extricate ourselves from situations, even ones that are already spent. It is the witch who initiates the transformative process; she protects her passengers as she ferries them across and the dream of the shore draws near.

THE WITCH'S SPELLS

POSITIVE: transition, personal transformation, travel

NEGATIVE: excessive attachment to the past, escape from problems

SEVEN OF SWORDS

In the Seven of Swords, the witch sneaks away with five Swords, leaving two behind, perhaps because she is in a hurry or she is afraid of being caught. She may be a spy or a thief who steals her enemies' weapons because she needs them; or maybe she wants to resolve her problems at any cost, regardless of adverse circumstances. She is clever, but she does not have much time. She deceives in order to survive. Plot twist: like all artists who use trickery to tell the truth.

THE WITCH'S SPELLS

POSITIVE: cunning, strategy, unusual perspectives, partial solutions

NEGATIVE: subterfuge, ambiguity, self-deception, lies, simulation

EIGHT OF SWORDS

The witch is tied and blindfolded, surrounded by swords, but all of them are stuck in the ground. Her feet and mouth are free; she could cry for help. What is really stopping her? In the Eight of Swords, we take stock of the negativity around us but we must also face our self-imposed limits and the severity with which we judge ourselves, imagining that we are both guilty and the victims of everything. One step, one deep breath is all it takes. Our insecurities are not the end of the world.

THE WITCH'S SPELLS

POSITIVE: abandoning negative thoughts, facing fears, liberating surrender

NEGATIVE: victim complex, excessive self-criticism, gossip, paralysis

NINE OF SWORDS

However you read it, the Nine of Swords is a card of pain. The witch awakens from a nightmare, crying. The real world and her inner anxiety mix, blurring the lines between one and the other. Her mind is confused and her chest is heavy. The cause of her suffering is unimportant. Suffering takes each part of us and twists it. In order to react, particularly in this case, you must accept the situation and then save yourself with any means possible. Ask for help.

THE WITCH'S SPELLS

POSITIVE: painful awakening, hope through acceptance

NEGATIVE: nightmares, persistent pain, shock, anxiety, depression

TEN OF SWORDS

In Tarot cards, nothing can be hidden and nothing can be saved. Alternating luck, teachings, gifts and tears, ruin and desperation, the lowest point in our lives, when we are so exhausted that we believe we cannot go on. The witch in the Ten of Swords represents all of these. She lies on the bank, pierced by a sword, a cycle that has ended dramatically. The end has prevailed on hope, yet at times something is so completely finished that it can survive only in illusions. Wake up to a new self. The sea is calm and the storm is over.

THE WITCH'S SPELLS

<u>POSITIVE:</u> lessons learned, necessary ending, melodrama

<u>NEGATIVE:</u> desperation, tragedy, bitterness, ruin

PAGE OF SWORDS

The wren flies off to tell the Page of Swords what it has seen. Perhaps the wren adds a few details, but its passion is such that its story is overwhelming. The Page listens, ready for action. He certainly has no lack of curiosity or spirit of adventure, and he has a way with words and a dose of rebelliousness against the system. He sharpens his tongue before his sword, but sometimes he sharpens it too much and a piece of truth gets lost on the wayside. Not all lies are harmful, though. After all, even fairy tales and poetry are a trickery of words, but they allow us to survive in dark times.

THE WITCH'S SPELLS

POSITIVE: curiosity, vigilance, readiness, mental dexterity, communication

NEGATIVE: treachery, cynicism, distraction, lack of logic

KNIGHT OF SWORDS

The witch plunges toward earth, riding on the back of the raven of thought. She unsheathes her sword without hesitation and her goal is clear. The Knight of Swords comes to our aid when we have to pursue an objective, filling us with temerity and determination, even if at times he risks being overly aggressive and getting caught up in the pure pleasure of the action. But for the time being, let's follow the witch on her flight. She and the raven's eye are one, convinced and compelling. She implies that anything can happen if your will is strong and you refuse to be influenced by outside factors.

THE WITCH'S SPELLS

POSITIVE: temerity, daring leadership, future vision, assertiveness, honesty

NEGATIVE: arrogance, impulsiveness, lack of direction, ambition-induced blindness

QUEEN OF SWORDS

At the top of the castle that rises up from the mountain, the Queen of Swords sits on her regal throne, cleaning the blood from her sword. Battle has brought her wisdom, through defeat and victory, through the bitterness and the fleeting sweetness of triumph. At her feet lie the apples from an ancient tree, the prohibited fruit of knowledge, the fruit that reveals the truth and poisons youth. This queen has tasted it and given it out. She has won back the purity of heart she lost in the evil and the vices of the world. Her companion is an ermine, whose fur changes color with the seasons. It represents a mind that has been purified through sacrifice, research, and experience; if you have one at your side, you have the best possible guide.

THE WITCH'S SPELLS

POSITIVE: perception, clarity of vision, liberating strength

NEGATIVE: indifference, lack of affection, cruelty

KING OF SWORDS

The stark kingdom of the King of Swords is made of wind, snow, and ice. The King goes where others do not dare, believing in the rationality that penetrates the physical and allows us to survive in the most hostile of times and places. He gets his spirit of adaptation to his surroundings from the arctic fox. This King calls for our accountability toward ourselves and others and invites us to look for an objective explanation for life's events. He may seem cold and distant, but he never gives up on his commitments. His demanding nature is outweighed by his sense of responsibility for the weak.

THE WITCH'S SPELLS

<u>POSITIVE</u>: intellectual strength, planning, rationality, authority, insight

<u>NEGATIVE</u>: lack of scruples, indifference, manipulation, irrationality

ACE OF PENTACLES

The elements of existence, air, water, fire, earth, and spirit, meet in the Ace of Pentacles. The witch explores them and looks for the borders where they come together. They represent magic in its first and ultimate purpose, to prosper in the world of senses and feelings, which have always been one—to work, dedicated to a new world made of sharing, loyalty, and widespread well-being. The witch plants the Ace, like a seed, among the flowers.

THE WITCH'S SPELLS

POSITIVE: new projects, resources, accomplishments, stability, opportunity

NEGATIVE: bad investments, missed opportunities, materialism

TWO OF PENTACLES

The witch of the Two of Pentacles is an able juggler who can do many things at once, even in complicated situations. In fact, as the sea is rising at her back, as fortunes interchange and challenges increase, the witch dances, making the sign of infinity. She can navigate multiple problems as long as she maintains her personal balance. Her dance expresses the levity with which we must face life, even when events bring instability to our environment.

THE WITCH'S SPELLS

POSITIVE: getting by, flexibility, adaptability, balance

NEGATIVE: chaos, lack of organization, sacrifices for stability

THREE OF PENTACLES

Three witches—one apprentice and two architects or clients—work together to finish a new project: a cathedral where everyone, not just humans, will be welcome regardless of their beliefs. Its doors will be open to terrestrial families with paws or wings, leaves, filaments, fins, or arms. The Three of Pentacles focuses on the value of cooperation between diverse cultures and wisdom. True knowledge is an encounter where experiences flow together and complete and color one another.

THE WITCH'S SPELLS

POSITIVE: work, collaboration, commissioning, collective wellbeing

NEGATIVE: disorganization, conflict of interests

FOUR OF PENTACLES

The witch of the Four of Pentacles holds tightly on to her material belongings. All of the cards have both negative and positive aspects, but this card is one of the most ambiguous. On the negative side is the longing for possession to its own end that we can find in every sphere of shared life, but on the positive side we see the comfort we get from the things most dear to us, those we use to build our haven. Old collections, books, fantasies, companions, and friends, even imaginary ones.

THE WITCH'S SPELLS

POSITIVE: haven, wealth, material stability, savings

NEGATIVE: avarice, possessiveness, waste of resources

FIVE OF PENTACLES

Two witches struggle in the freezing cold. They are poor and infirm and perhaps they could knock on the door of the church we see here, or perhaps they found the door closed so they tried knocking on the window. The primary sense of the Five of Pentacles is desolation. The card indicates situations in which we feel abandoned, disgraced, and in extreme economical or emotional difficulty, but it also suggests that in our most fragile moments, we must ask for help. We must forgive ourselves for the times we are unable to carry on using only our own strength.

THE WITCH'S SPELLS

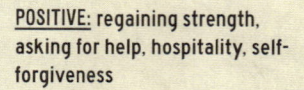

POSITIVE: regaining strength, asking for help, hospitality, self-forgiveness

NEGATIVE: desolation, disgrace, alienation, loss, abandonment

SIX OF PENTACLES

The witch of the Six of Pentacles uses one hand to give gifts to the needy and the other to hold up a scale, the symbol of justice. The two beggars open their hands and accept her charity with gratitude. Each of us could be any of the three figures on the card, a giver or a receiver; in order for the giver to give, the receiver must be able to receive and recognize the gift. This exchange, which is unequal in material substance, becomes equal at a spiritual level. True generosity never exaggerates; it re-creates equality.

THE WITCH'S SPELLS

POSITIVE: munificence, making good use of gifts, material support, giving and receiving

NEGATIVE: ingratitude, inequality, exploitation

SEVEN OF PENTACLES

In the Seven of Pentacles, the witch stops to rest after strenuous work. She contemplates the work she has done, knowing that there is much more to do. She is just beginning to see the first fruits, but she is not in a hurry. The more she enjoys the anticipation of her harvest, complying with the rhythms and ripening times of the season, the more rich and pleasing it will be. Commitment and patience guarantee success, as long as we relax every now and then and allow our minds to wander elsewhere.

THE WITCH'S SPELLS

POSITIVE: profitable commitment, investment, long-term predictions, harvest

NEGATIVE: haste, limited success, impatience

EIGHT OF PENTACLES

The witch of the Eight of Pentacles concentrates on her work as though it is one of the most enjoyable of jobs. No one can distract her. She is cultivating her inner child, for whom play is a very serious thing, and, at the same time, takes full responsibility for the success of her endeavor. She is capable, persevering, humble, and satisfied. She is never bored, nor does she worry if she will be recognized for her work. After all, every result is the sum total of its details, of quality, and of daily focus.

THE WITCH'S SPELLS

POSITIVE: care, quality, competence, concentration on the job, ability

NEGATIVE: lack of quality, mediocrity, work without results, lack of motivation

NINE OF PENTACLES

The stag comes out of the woods to visit an old acquaintance. It is the witch in the Nine of Pentacles. She is sitting peacefully in her garden, surrounded by the things she loves and absorbed by the magic of the book that tells the story of the stag. All private wealth is nourished with the gratitude of what comes from without. The witch is comfortable in her own company and with the things that surround her, but we must remember that when one book closes, a blank page opens.

THE WITCH'S SPELLS

POSITIVE: personal space, reached goal, material security, self-sufficiency

NEGATIVE: living beyond your means, superficiality

TEN OF PENTACLES

In the Ten of Pentacles, witches, big and small, are happy and safe, protected by the walls of their village and their house. Material well-being makes emotional unity stronger; the traditional values of family and home shine positively and illuminate a place to happily return to, where there is economical and emotional support. The witches live in a house that they built with dedication and an eye for the future, and present and future generations will reap the benefits.

THE WITCH'S SPELLS

POSITIVE: domestic happiness, inheritance, financial security, family, home

NEGATIVE: closed-mindedness, material attachment, fights about economic issues

PAGE OF PENTACLES

"What is there to learn?" asks the Page of Pentacles as he approaches a burning pentacle, a symbol of experience. He has one hand in the shadows because all knowledge is the revelation of further ignorance. His face is covered by a mask; he knows his apprenticeship will be slow and cautious, despite his enthusiasm. Too much fire burns instead of illuminating. Nature reawakens when he passes by with his companion, the badger, a symbol of perseverance, because his wisdom passes through his body and through the practicality of what we can cultivate in a continuous relationship between ourselves and the earth.

THE WITCH'S SPELLS

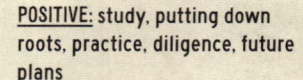

POSITIVE: study, putting down roots, practice, diligence, future plans

NEGATIVE: lack of vision, absence of prospects, laziness, pretention

KNIGHT OF PENTACLES

The Knight of Pentacles has no interest in being the first to arrive. He rides his friend, the peacock, the symbol of protection and renewal. The animal's colors are reminiscent of the many shades of nature that the Knight stops to admire. He knows that beauty comes from dedication and details, brush stroke after brush stroke, and that, syllable by syllable, a poem takes shape. No matter where he goes, he chooses to go slowly and avoids shortcuts. Certainly it is important to look ahead, but it is no less important to leave traces of yourself in your surroundings and welcome the ordinary wonders of the path.

THE WITCH'S SPELLS

POSITIVE: practical sense, respect for nature, devotion, diligence

NEGATIVE: boredom, addiction to work, lack of initiative

QUEEN OF PENTACLES

The Queen of Pentacles has everything. She is the queen of abundance and of the self-love that makes it possible to embrace others without fear. She has learned to cherish the gifts she has and makes no distinction between the joys of the body and those of the spirit. She is accompanied by a red wolf, the color of autumn when it gives us the gift of its harvest. The wolf, like the queen, is sustained by beauty, and he shares it with whoever learns to ask. The Tarot cards ask us to appreciate our resources and to put down roots in ourselves and in our spaces. The most intriguing elsewhere is right here, where we grow.

THE WITCH'S SPELLS

POSITIVE: material care, generosity, abundance, sex life

NEGATIVE: intolerance, jealousy, adulation

KING OF PENTACLES

The King of Pentacles is the embodiment of the earth's ancestor, of the material, of the wood that grows, ring by ring, in the tree's trunk. He accumulates wealth and turns every clump of dirt into a profit. He does not leave things as they are; he intervenes knowingly. He remembers that woods where we love to wander are born from the collaboration between man and plants. This Ancestor-King is an able forester and shares his experience with the places where he roams. His companion and alter ego, the Stag King, enriches the King's practical sense with the sensuality of the woods and a contemplative spirit.

THE WITCH'S SPELLS

POSITIVE: security, material wealth, protection, prosperity

NEGATIVE: exploitation, speculation, avarice

READING AND INTERPRETING THE TAROT CARDS

BECOMING COMFORTABLE WITH THE CARDS

In this chapter, you will find indications about how to consult your deck of cards and ask the witches for advice. The first thing to do is to get familiar with the images; not all of them will be immediately visible. Look at the cards in any order you like; look at their details and read their meanings. I suggest starting with the cards that most strongly attract you or repel you, because those are certainly the ones with which you will best interact and that will open an interpretive pathway that will guide you toward the others. As you read the information in the book, let your mind wander: Do you recognize someone or something in the card in front of you? Do you want to add a word or focus on one particular detail? Remember that there are no wrong ideas. Tarot cards work as gateways to interior worlds and present and future developments, and every reader forges his or her own personal access key. Use the book any way you like; underline and take notes, and make it into a magical object of your own. Keep a log where you write down your impressions of the cards and their combinations. If some do not speak to you, do not get discouraged, it is only a question of time, practice, and even luck. If they suggest strange or unexpected combinations, accept them. Every card will reveal its importance to your life when the time is right.

CREATE YOUR OWN SPACE

Creating a space where you read your cards is important, but not always possible. Some of us carry our cards around in our bag, for example, and peek at them while we ride the subway or the bus, or on a work break or at a table in a café. In such cases, you can create a mental space where you can be alone with your cards, even if it is only for a few minutes. If you are at home, unlimited by time or other commitments, you can prepare your space calmly. You can make yourself a cup of coffee or tea, lay out herbs and crystals if you use them, and light a few candles or some incense. Or maybe you prefer a simpler, more essential space.

Do whatever makes you completely comfortable and get ready to cross the threshold of images. When you feel ready, concentrate on the question you want to ask the cards. Keep in mind that the cards do not give answers to blunt yes-or-no questions; divination with Tarot cards depends on the story that is told by the meeting between the images and your interpretation of them; and, as we know, stories do not begin with the ending. Look for the path rather than the solution; ask for help to see clearly.

Remember, too, that witches should be approached with caution. Formulate your question and brace yourself for a fascinating and sometimes enigmatic response that will reflect your life, but from the perspective of magic. You have to be completely willing to take a risk. Now, shuffle the cards and choose your spread.

SPREADS

A spread is the method used to read the cards, laid out in a precise order. Every spread has its own meanings and every card must be read according to its position in the spread. For example, if you find the Sun as an obstacle, you cannot focus on the general positivity associated with the card; you have to consider its negative aspects, which are blindness, the discovery of a painful truth, temporary success, and failure. In the same way, the Five of Pentacles in a positive or helpful position should be read as an ally who will guarantee aid and a way out of difficult personal and economic situations.

The Card of the Day

The first spread, the Daily Card, is actually a constant practice. Choose one card from the deck in the morning or the evening, or whenever you can at some point during the day. If you pick the same card from the deck more than once in a short period of time, take note: it is trying to tell you something important. For example, during stressful periods or times of emotional, physical, or mental fatigue, you may find the Four of Swords, which means you should rest and call a truce so you can focus your attention solely on your own recovery. Use your free time to enjoy your peace and do not fill it with other activities. Your intuition will tell you if the card you pull is reversed, in which case you must consider its negative aspects.

Three-Card Spread

The most popular and widely used spread is the Three-Card Spread. The following are a variety of ways to lay out the cards.

1. Present. Past. Future.
The first card is in the middle and represents the present. The

second, on the left, is the past that led to the current situation, and the third is future development.

2. Situation. Obstacle. Overcoming.
From the left, the first card represents the situation you want to address. The second is the obstacle you must face, and the third is how it will (or will not) be overcome.

3. Situation. Shadow Aspects. Strong Points.
Lay the cards out in a vertical line. The first, in the middle, is the situation you want to investigate. The second card, on the bottom, shows the shadow, or hidden, elements—problems or things you have difficulty coming to terms with. The third, on the top, shows your qualities, which become your strong points.

The Witch's Harvest

I created a spread specifically for this deck, which you can use to interrogate the witches directly. Every witch is also a healer who often uses herbs and other natural substances for her spells, just like Biddy Early in the Temperance card.

When you use this spread, imagine that you are a witch getting ready to prepare one of her potions with the ingredients gathered from the garden, in the woods, along the riverbank, at the seashore, or even walking along the sidewalk, among the bricks and the flowers that grow stubbornly out of the concrete.

Take your deck in your hands, whisper your words, entrust your fate to the heart's cup, to the wand's dream, to the truth's sword, and to the pentacle's wisdom; then get ready for the harvest.

Shuffle your cards, choose six of them, and lay them out according to the drawing:

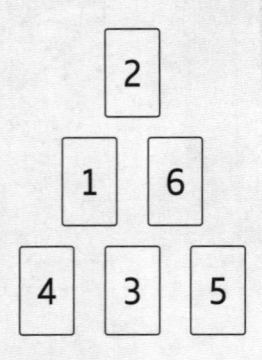

```
        2

    1       6

  4     3     5
```

1. **SITUATION.** The situation you want to examine.
2. **MAGIC.** Personal magic, or the place to look for advice; the qualities that give you your power.
3. **SHADOW.** Difficult, hidden elements that you will have to face.
4. **RESIDUAL.** That which can be left behind, that you do not need for development.
5. **HARVEST.** That which can be harvested and used. The fruit of your efforts.
6. **TRANSFORMATION.** Future events. Possible evolution of the initial situation and of your harvest.

Use this spread to explore events in every aspect, including your soul. What happens inside you holds the vastness of the cosmos. The witches are here to facilitate the meeting of the worlds.

THE WITCHES' MESSAGES

MAJOR ARCANA

0 The Fool – Crazy Jane
"Sometimes it is in letting yourself fall that you learn to fly. One step on the ground and another in the air, where the rainbow begins and, in an instant, your arms turn to wings."

I The Magician – Circe
"Magic is an illusion for skeptics and cosmic unity for seekers. Sharpen your tools and your potential. Become one with your dreams and then let them scatter."

II The High Priestess – Cumaean Sybil
"Let the images that spring from within you rise to the surface. Repeat their foreign tongue, which is also yours. It speaks to you of the earth and of the ancestors. Welcome it and cherish it."

III The Empress – Ceridwen
"Dedicate yourself as a mother, a sister, fertile terrain, and a fertile mind for your world. Create it, cultivate it and lead it. Only then can you imagine others, rich, generous, and full of joy."

IV The Emperor – Morgan le Fay
"Will is never consumed in the present; it sees far away and is very patient. Know your sovereignty; it is a gift from the Earth around which everything rotates."

V The Hierophant – Saraswati
"Listen and observe. Walk in the footsteps of those who came before you. Only then will your steps have the right substance to mark a new path. Yours."

VI The Lovers – Titania
"What does it mean to love? In love, let others disarm you and experience you. Accept what is strange, the strength, find joy in the small shared things. Embrace your nature in others."

VII The Chariot – Holda
"Existence is a voyage to an un-

known destination. While you plan where to go, be curious about the things and the beings you will meet along the way. Hold out your hand. Enjoy the slowness."

VIII Strength – Joan of Arc
"Your vulnerability is your strength. Remember that courage is born from the knowledge of fear. True defeat is to betray our inner fragility, where the world appears."

IX The Hermit – The Witch of Endor
"Your imagination will give you the light to see your way. Walk as a guide and a mother atop the mountain that is blocking your path. In your solitude, discover the voice of a multitude of beings."

X The Wheel of Fortune – The Fates
"Destiny is a great work, a wheel where highs and lows alternate and blend. You cannot stop the Wheel. Learn to turn in her. Call the changes revelations."

XI Justice – Sedna
"Act with compassion. That which looks unjust now may reveal its reasons in the future. In the meantime, be supportive with all beings. Practice inner and cosmic justice."

XII The Hanged Man – Luonnotar
"Change your views and give birth to a sacred dream. Live in the invisible; perform a ritual. Substitute action with waiting and contemplation. Let things appear, springing from the essence."

XIII Death – Baba Yaga
"Prepare yourself for transformation. You die many times over in one existence, regenerating the skin that has become useless. Get closer to the center. Let one cycle feed another and let the worlds touch."

XIV Temperance – Biddy Early
"Combine what you are with what you have and your potential with your exterior. Safeguard your shadow because goodness flows from it. And in the goodness, recognize the shadows of others."

XV The Devil – Lilith
"Descend into the wild, in your rebellion. Let it impassion you. Get lost only to find yourself again; do not let a pathway take your soul. Remember that the soul is a demon. Decide how to listen to it."

XVI The Tower – Oya
"When things collapse, they redesign the landscape. If something no longer exists now, you must get used to its absence. The power that destroys creates an opening, in pain and in possibility."

XVII The Star – Aradia
"Hope wears away at the rock until it reduces it to grass, earth, and seeds. Remember to believe in yourself; and when you feel you can no longer manage, look up at the lights outside. Be confident."

XVIII The Moon – Hecate
"The life you live in your night dreams gives you precious insight into your daytime life and your spirit. Do not run from the insight. Shine the torch of time on it. Use it to sweep away your illusions."

XIX The Sun – Bastet
"Rejoice simply because you are present in this life! Colors are blooming everywhere, puppies are playing everywhere, and beauty can answer suddenly, everywhere. All things are illuminated by joy."

XX Judgment – Befana
"In forgiveness, in reconciliation, in the call to your deepest vocation, to your talent, to your inner voice, in the choir of the lives you love and have loved, in the gift of a new breath. Arise."

XXI The World – Xiwangmu
"You are home now. Nothing can hurt you; everything can change radically, break you, give you new life. Every step is a return. Every dream come true is the end of a world. Or the beginning."

MINOR ARCANA

Wands

Ace of Wands
"I am the fire and the magic wand; the creativity, the spark of life, the imagination that travels beyond the limits."

Two of Wands
"Look at the horizon and design the world. Start with the small winged seed in your hand, and prepare it for a favorable wind."

Three of Wands
"Begin a journey in your mind. Sharpen your senses: the horizon begins with your understanding of the signs and the seasons."

Four of Wands
"Celebrate every goal. Before a journey, take time to say good-bye to what is dear to you."

Five of Wands
"Join forces with others; do not engage in futile conflict. Reach an agreement for a common goal."

Six of Wands
"You have traveled far to prove your worth, which is finally acknowledged; curiosity, empathy, and humility guarantee a happy return."

Seven of Wands
"Defend what is yours: dignity, talent, choices. Head held high and an open mind: your clarity is the strongest armor."

Eight of Wands
"Transform every message into a seed for your life. Seize the moment. Everything happens now and always."

Nine of Wands
"Stand on the side of what you love, no matter how small. All things require a special kind of courage."

Ten of Wands
"Do not make useless sacrifices. The battle is over; let go of what you no longer need. Lighten your load."

Page of Wands
"I am curiosity, invention, and play. I get excited for every small thing that I create with my imagination."

Knight of Wands
"I dream big for myself and others. My charisma leads the crowds. I rewrite the rules with a touch of genius."

Queen of Wands
"The witch that lives in me does what she wants, for whim or for will. I speak my mind and smile at those who are fragile. Do not follow me. Follow my example."

King of Wands
"I can decide, lead, and see solutions where others fumble in the dark. If I fall, I reinvent myself. I regain control."

Cups

Ace of Cups
"I am the water and the cup of the heart: sentiment, devotion, and the love in which we are reborn, together with others."

Two of Cups
"Sometimes two become one, recognizing one another. Reach your soul and embrace it through another."

Three of Cups
"Find your community, like an intertwining of souls and trust. Family is not where you are born, but where you settle."

Four of Cups
"Accept what has been and open your eyes to what is offered. Lighten your spirit. Each of us has a place in the world."

Five of Cups
"Live the season of loss. As you say good-bye, appreciate what remains and what awaits you."

Six of Cups
"Nourish yourself with memories. Cultivate your childhood, not as a place of escape, but as an innocent look at time."

Seven of Cups
"Let your fantasies flow freely, then shine a light on them with your intuition. Distinguish dreams from illusions."

Eight of Cups
"When the time to depart comes, wear your soul like a skin made of courage. Seek your dreams with no fear of losing yourself."

Nine of Cups
"When the soul's cups are full, have a party and share them. Pour them into others and into your future lives, with gratitude."

Ten of Cups
"All things are blessed by love. In love, no one is judged. Raise your eyes to the magnificence and carry it within you."

Page of Cups
"I am sensitivity, dreams, innocence. I fall in love with words, leaves, and gazes. I give inspiration."

Knight of Cups
"I travel along my fairy tale path. I am ready to know the forest for love. At times, my ideals surpass reality."

Queen of Cups
"I will soothe your wounds. I have already been in loss, sufferance, and fear. I leave the mark of awareness and healing as I wash the evil from my memory."

King of Cups
"I know the sea of sentiments. It does not sweep me away. I help others find their way. My mind is in my heart and my heart is in my mind."

Swords

Ace of Swords
"I am the air and the sword of truth: the mind, the clarity of vision and the intellect that dispels the fog of life."

Two of Swords
"Establish a mental space where your inner truth can come out. At times you can see better with your eyes closed."

Three of Swords
"Do you think you cannot survive the pain? Your heart is pierced but it is whole. Let the trials you face regenerate you. The scar is a pathway to help you get over it."

Four of Swords
"It is time for resting and healing. Retire to your den and recover your strength. You will find solutions in your sleep."

Five of Swords
"That which is forced on us does not last. Expose yourself to defeat. In bitterness, you will find the patience to go on."

Six of Swords
"As you travel toward unknown shores, look for an able guide. Or bravely protect and accompany others as they cross."

Seven of Swords
"I continue along my backward way. I imagine a plan to survive. I prefer secrecy to open battle."

Eight of Swords
"When you cannot see what you have around you, use your other senses, including the inner ones. Stay calm and look for a way out."

Nine of Swords
"Your suffering wakes you up during the night. Take a breath. I offer no solution. Stop. Ask for help. Let time go by."

Ten of Swords
"I frighten you, I know. Because I am the end. Look the other way, at another sun that is rising."

Page of Swords
"I am the quick-of-tongue who twists the plot of the story I tell. I am vigilant and able and I rewrite the story to make it true."

Knight of Swords
"I establish my goal and I rush to reach it. I can do what I want; I express myself with daring. Every now and then, my intentions are damaged by my impulsiveness."

Queen of Swords
"I acquired my knowledge in battle. Defeat has accompanied me like a dearest friend. Expect the truth from me, not pity."

King of Swords
"Reason guides me as I carry out my plans. My power is in the lucidity of thought. I am not in a hurry."

Pentacles

Ace of Pentacles
"I am the earth and the pentacle of reason: complete stability, the matter in which all things come true and become aware of themselves."

Two of Pentacles
"The world evolves in dance. Your dream and your body are the center into which everything flows."

Three of Pentacles
"Working in a group stimulates your imagination; it reinvigorates the soul and generates new ideas, giving your work the benefit of the meeting between different views."

Four of Pentacles
"Material belongings are a comfort. Do not let them become a cage;

learn to live without them when it is necessary."

Five of Pentacles
"Ask for help in times of need. You no longer have physical strength, but you still have a voice with which to tell your story."

Six of Pentacles
"Those who give make a pact with those who receive. The mutual acceptance by both parties means knowing that every condition is uncertain."

Seven of Pentacles
"Gather your fruits when the time comes; follow the seasons without haste. Imagine the beauty that is to come."

Eight of Pentacles
"Pay attention and respect to the details. Often, that is where the longest-lasting qualities of things make their nest."

Nine of Pentacles
"Develop your personal space, dedicate yourself to something you love, and regain the serenity of the things that bring you pleasure."

Ten of Pentacles
"Enjoy domestic happiness, the things you have created with those dear to you. But never forget that the world is waiting, outside."

Page of Pentacles
"I am the desire for experience. You can recognize me in every creature that learns to walk, to read, and to create connections between things learned."

Knight of Pentacles
"On my journey, I stop to talk to the creatures I meet. Their messages better me. The path itself is my destination."

Queen of Pentacles
"I give the gift of abundance with every gesture. In me, you can learn to love yourself and share your resources with others. You grow in all places. You become your own 'here.'"

King of Pentacles
"I guarantee security and well-being. I protect those who ask me for shelter. I bring prosperity to my world and those who belong to it. All are welcome."

FRANCESCA MATTEONI

A poet, writer, and historian, Francesca Matteoni earned her doctorate degree in England, where she also conducted research about witches' trials, the magic of heavenly bodies, and medical folklore. She conducts workshops on Tarot cards and poetry and teaches the history of religions and magic at the American University in Florence. Her most recent publications include the essay *Dal Matto al Mondo* (effequ, 2019), a poetic voyage into the world of Tarot cards, the poetic text *Libro di Hor* (Vydia, 2019), with illustrations by Ginevra Ballati, and a contribution to the collective book *La Scommessa Psichedelica* (Quodlibet, 2020), edited by Federico Di Vita.

SIMONE PACE

Simone Pace is an illustrator and cartoonist with a degree in Cartoon Languages from the Academy of Fine Arts in Bologna. He is an enthusiast of medieval culture, magic, and fantasy, all of which he ably blends in his drawings. His colorful pop style is reminiscent of the Japanese tradition of anime and European cartoons, but with his own personal, original touch. He published the graphic novel *Anguisomachia* for Barta Edizioni, and he collaborates with a number of editors and magazines. He is also the founding member of the cartoonist organization Sciame.

ROCKPOOL

A Rockpool book
PO Box 252
Summer Hill NSW 2130
Australia

rockpoolpublishing.co

Follow us! f © rockpoolpublishing
Tag your images with #rockpoolpublishing

Originally published by Vivida Books, a trademark of White Star s.r.l.

This edition published by Rockpool Publishing, 2021

ISBN: 9781922579300

Copyright text and artwork © 2021 White Star s.r.l.
Design by Davide Canesi / PEPE nymi
Translation: ICEIGeo, Milan: Cynthia Anne Koeppe - Editing: Phillip Gaskill

Printed and bound in China

10 9 8 7 6 5 4 3 2 1

All rights reserved. No part of this publication may be reproduced, stored in a retrieval system, or transmitted in any form or by any means, electronic, mechanical, photocopying, recording or otherwise, without the prior written permission of the publisher.

Editorial conception and coordination: Balthazar Pagani